The Global Shelter Imaginary

Forerunners: Ideas First

Short books of thought-in-process scholarship, where intense analysis, questioning, and speculation take the lead

FROM THE UNIVERSITY OF MINNESOTA PRESS

(Continued on page 66)

The Global Shelter Imaginary

IKEA Humanitarianism and Rightless Relief

Daniel Bertrand Monk and Andrew Herscher

University of Minnesota Press

MINNEAPOLIS

LONDON

ISBN 978-1-5179-1222-2 (PB)
ISBN 978-1-4529-6602-1 (Ebook)
ISBN 978-1-4529-6655-7 (Manifold)

Published by the University of Minnesota Press
111 Third Avenue South, Suite 290
Minneapolis, MN 55401–2520
http://www.upress.umn.edu

▧ Available as a Manifold edition at manifold.umn.edu

The University of Minnesota is an equal-opportunity educator and employer.

In Memory of Daniel Moses Herscher
and Raquel Helman Monk

Contents

Preface and Acknowledgments

THE GLOBAL SHELTER IMAGINARY is, in part, a response to arguments previously advanced by its own authors. In an essay concerning the way that architectural and humanitarian discourses have each labored to dissociate the concept of refuge from that of the refugee we sought to show how each domain has turned the other into a kind of compensatory form.[1] In humanitarian thought, we maintained, shelter becomes a fetish for threatened rights, and in architectural discourse novel forms of relief become substitutes for a shelter that is nowhere really on offer. As time passed, however, we came to see this same argument as an intuitive but inadequate step toward describing an empirical—though abstract—reality. We began to understand that the role we had accorded to architecture in humanitarian reason was itself an effect of contemporary humanitarian reason. Indeed, however counterintuitive it may appear at first glance, the argument elaborated in the following pages is that the humanitarian order's investment in architecture normalizes its disinvestment in the protection of the dispossessed.

It took us a while and a great deal of research to develop these arguments. We would like to express our thanks to Lucia Allais and Zeynep Çelik, editors of the journal *Grey Room*, for giving us the opportunity to test-drive the early versions of what has become

---

1. Monk and Herscher, "The New Universalism."

a work of profound importance for us. Equally, we would like to thank Anooradha Iyer Siddiqi, Ijlal Muzaffar, Mark Jarzombeck, and Miriam Ticktin for their meaningful contributions to a refuge/refugee round table published in the same venue. They spurred us to continue onward. Conversations with Romain Desclous, of UNHCR, and Märta Terne, of BetterShelter.org, also proved invaluable.

Initial drafts of *The Global Shelter Imaginary* were written at the Montalvo Center in Saratoga, California, where the authors made use of the time and space offered by a Lucas Program Fellowship to reframe the work. Without the kindness and support of Montalvo's Kelly Sicat and Lori Wood, we would not have been able to find the time or place to collaborate so effectively. They are probably unaware of it, but a number of conversations with Laurie Anderson, Karrie Hovey, and Kio Griffiths during the period of the Lucas Fellowship greatly helped us to refine the argument. Drafts of the resulting text were presented before colleagues in the academy. We are grateful to Ana Teixeira Pinto for giving us the opportunity to present the project at the Porto Design Biennial, and to the Colgate University Social Science Faculty workshops for a chance to discuss its argument in draft form. We would also like thank Antoine Bousquet, Romola Sanyal, and Ayça Çubukçu for inviting us to present portions of this study at the London School of Economics' Human Rights Centre. Equally, we are grateful to Aggie Hirst, Paul Kirby, Charlotte Heath-Kelly, and Oren Yiftachel for their probing questions during that event. If we still messed up, it is our fault entirely. They did their best.

In the course of writing *The Global Shelter Imaginary*, each of the authors suffered the loss of a parent. We dedicate this work to them.

Introduction: The Global Shelter Imaginary

He who wishes to know the truth about life in its immediacy
must scrutinize its estranged form . . .

—THEODOR W. ADORNO, *Minima Moralia: Reflections
from a Damaged Life*

When . . . an international body arrogated itself a nongov-
ernmental authority, its failure was apparent even before its
measures were realized.

—HANNAH ARENDT, *The Origins of Totalitarianism*

IN LATE APRIL 2019 an official of the United Nations Refugee
Agency (UNHCR) traveled to north-central Burkina Faso in order
to report on the status of people forcibly displaced by an ongoing
conflict between the state and Islamist forces. Visiting a site for
internally displaced persons in Barsologho, the official also pho-
tographed his own agency's efforts to assist some of the 150,000
people forced to flee their homes by the spring of that year. (Within
twelve months the number would reach one million). As he doc-
umented the resettlement of 1400 people displaced by attacks on
the village of Yirgou, in particular, the official took a snapshot of
an impromptu dwelling made from the same cardboard boxes in
which a new, standard, UNHCR refugee housing unit (RHU) deployed to the region had been packed.[1] More specifically, someone

1. UN High Commissioner for Refugees, "Conflict, Violence in
Burkina Faso Displaces Nearly Half a Million People"; Romain Desclous

Figure 1. Cardboard packaging from the IKEA Foundation–supported Better Shelter Flat-Pak emergency shelter has been used to provide shade at a site for internally displaced persons. April 30, 2019. Photograph copyright UNHCR/Romain Desclous.

had cribbed together a shelter of last resort out of the flat-pack containers that had held a "Better Shelter," a new humanitarian concept dwelling sponsored by the UNHCR in partnership with the IKEA Foundation.

If the photograph records the insufficiency of global humanitarianism's best efforts, the image simultaneously exhumes the

(spokesperson for UNHCR in West Africa) in discussion with the authors, Zoom, August 24, 2020.

workings of a broader social imaginary.[2] On one hand, the image directs the viewer's empathy toward a "lesser evil principle," on the premise that any shelter is better than no shelter. On the other hand, the imaginary of which it is a part offers up *those* sentiments as artifacts of a species of humanitarian governance that has successfully normalized "lesser evil" rationalizations to begin with. According to this latter view, sedimented in the photograph's pixels are traces of a political process whereby the protection of refugees and the displaced has been abandoned in favor of a generalized preoccupation with relief logistics.

To understand how the humanitarian order could betray a mandate in the appearance of its fulfillment one would have to know the conditions under which refugee protection has come to be understood instead as a "mere problem of residence."[3] Three international agreements punctuate the contemporary history of global refugee management: the UN General Assembly's 2016 "New York Declaration for Refugees and Migrants," a subsequent "Global Compact on Refugees" in 2018, and then the first Global Refugee Forum in 2019. Viewed as an ensemble, these agreements are an effort not only to manage what stakeholders describe as a "global migration crisis" but, more consequentially, to shift the referent of this crisis from the refugee to the refuge.[4] With this transposition, longstanding apprehensions about the erosion of the world's juridical asylum architecture give way to questions about "burden sharing" and "third country solutions" as a way to "ease pressures on host countries."[5] In such a context, by dint of the sheer numbers of humans seeking asylum, the protections guaranteed to refugees under international conventions are assumed to be guaranteed

2. Taylor, *Modern Social Imaginaries*, 23.

3. Agier, *Managing the Undesirables*, 16.

4. For a symptomatic registration of this shift, see *Structures of Protection? Rethinking Refugee Shelter*, ed. Tom Scott-Smith and Mark E. Breeze.

5. UN High Commissioner for Refugees, "The Global Compact on Refugees."

by the notional inalienability of those rights to begin with. As a result, an established language of "protection" gives way to new pronouncements regarding refugee "dignity" and "self-reliance."[6]

Astute observers of the international refugee order have not failed to notice that there is a progressive abandonment and effacement of the dispossessed precisely as this order advances a new and nominally progressive jargon of care.[7] Here, as Didier Fassin explains, the "deployment of moral sentiments" constitutes a new species of "humanitarian government": "inequality is replaced by exclusion, domination is transformed into misfortune, injustice is articulated by suffering, violence is expressed in terms of trauma."[8]

Also referred to as "sentimental humanitarianism," the new humanitarian government inaugurates a "moral economy" that "mobilizes compassion rather than justice."[9] Tweeting the word counts of the UNHCR reports on each of the refugee compacts, for example, critics/scholars document how a key terminology of rights—words like "asylum" and "non-refoulement"—is giving way to repeated mentions of "detention" and "assistance."[10] Even more to the point, students of humanitarianism understand that this new "ethic of compassion" is actually directed toward a "privatized public," as the

6. UN High Commissioner for Refugees, "Global Compact on Refugees." The compact's four key objectives are: "Ease the pressures on host countries; Enhance refugee self-reliance; Expand access to third-country solutions; Support conditions in countries of origin for return in safety and dignity."

7. Jeff Crisp (@JFCrisp), "Phrases I won't be using in 2020: 'Global refugee crisis' 'Record number of refugees' 'One person displaced every two seconds' 'Persons of concern' 'Complementary pathways' 'Bringing refugees to the market' 'Private sector engagement' 'New paradigm' 'Gamechanger' 'Changemaker,'" Twitter post, December 24, 2019, 9:21 a.m., https://twitter.com/JFCrisp/status/1209388630550237190.

8. Fassin, *Humanitarian Reason,* 6.

9. Fassin, *Humanitarian Reason,* 7–8. For discussions of a sentimental humanitarianism, see Berlant and Warner, "Sex in Public"; Owens, "Xenophilia, Gender, and Sentimental Humanitarianism."

10. Crisp, "Phrases I won't be using in 2020."

humanitarian order transforms itself into a "neo-humanitarianism" largely premised on the privatization of public policy models and market-driven models of success.[11]

At the same time, however, this re-imagination of humanitarianism has also presupposed the elaboration of new legitimation horizons that have remained largely transparent to themselves. Believing that stakeholders in refugee management in turn believe that migration has triggered a self-evident state of emergency for the community of nations, observers of the current transformations in humanitarian governance have been less attentive to the emergence of a vision of assistance, not only ubiquitous but also normative, best described as a global shelter imaginary.

The term "global shelter imaginary" refers to a number of related concepts. First, it describes a generalized subordination of the refugee to the *given* image of refuge. That subordination of empirical refugees to representations of their plight may also be understood as a political morphology, in the sense that the representation of what is posed as the migration "crisis" already presupposes the *shape* of a response. In this instance, the "social construction of public problems" recruits/involves architecture–broadly conceived—as an answer to displacement: the global shelter imaginary retroactively presents the political problem of involuntary migration as if were part of a "housing question" instead.[12] Stated more directly, the global shelter imaginary is the way that the current humanitarian order treats architecture/shelter as a plenipotentiary for the political protections it is actually abandoning, and then frames the abandonment of the dispossessed as if it constituted a moral triumph—an act of rescue. The global shelter imaginary attains its social function by repeatedly transposing irreducible political quandaries into technocratic challenges.

11. Owens, "Xenophilia, Gender, and Sentimental Humanitarianism" 296. See also the chapter "Neo-humanitarianism" in Barnett, *Empire of Humanity*.

12. Bourdieu, *On the State*, 23.

The public career of the global shelter imaginary has been hiding in plain sight. This imaginary is vividly on display, for example, in the press releases, churnalism, and social media concerning the unprecedented partnership between the United Nations Refugee Agency [UNHCR] and the IKEA Foundation on the design and mass production of the same "better" refugee shelter encountered by the UN official in Burkina Faso. Indeed, a careful assessment of the public arguments for what would eventually be named and trademarked as Better Shelter lays bare the legitimation horizons of the current humanitarian order itself. Seemingly epiphenomenal to the scale of the misery it is designed to address, the Better Shelter is actually an essential cipher/artifact of the order that defines itself as the administrator of this same misery. A phenomenology of its place in the administered world of refugee governance points to the way that lesser-of-two-evils arguments—"since there are no other solutions we must make the dispossessed as comfortable as we can"—introduce and give way to valorizations of biopolitical governance *tout court*. Stated differently: a review of the attention economy surrounding commonplace proposals to resolve the so-called refugee conundrum by providing "refuge in displacement," discloses an underexamined regulative ideal concerning the proper "place" of the refugee within that economy.[13] This ideal is the global shelter imaginary—a place where the compromise of cosmopolitan right appears as the fulfillment of this right in the form of one or another "better shelter."

The key reflection advanced here is that the shift in priority toward technocratic responses to humanitarian problems constitutes an evasion of the political or, more specifically, an institutionally sanctioned politics of evasion whose own path toward the rationalization of rightless relief is outlined in pronouncements and speech acts on the status of architecture in humanitarian action. In the

13. Rajaram, "Humanitarianism and Representations of the Refugee," as cited in Haddad, *The Refugee in International Society,* 35. See also Rajaram, "Humanitarianism and Representations of the Refugee," in the *Journal of Refugee Studies.*

following, then, we trace how the concept of protection has been superseded by a language of assistance that takes form in unreflexive talk about the self-evident worth of better refugee shelters. *The Global Shelter Imaginary* outlines the normalization of this process in four discrete episodes.

Chapter 1, "Better Shelter / Better Refugee," interprets the decision of the UNHCR and IKEA to promote the development of a universal emergency shelter as a sociological event. Here, the humanitarian reputation of the UNHCR and the "smart" status of IKEA are effectively exchanged in the mutual adoption of the Better Shelter as a template of refugee relief. As they advance a new and shared image of the social good, the UNHCR and IKEA together promote a new sociodicy of relief in which shelter stands in for protection. Better Shelter talk paradoxically normalizes this substitution via the replacement of any mention of rights with repeated references to dignity. In the process, shelter talk valorizes rightless relief and the biopolitics this relief advances. The refugee thus becomes the adjunct of the given notion of refuge; a better shelter demands a better refugee, who must, paradoxically, be domesticated as a functionary of the global shelter imaginary in order to be recognized at all.

The transformations just described cast a new light on the history of the refugee camp, which is the subject of chapter 2, "There Has Always Been a Better Shelter." Whereas received studies of camp humanitarianism typically foreground the origins of the camp in colonial strategies of internment—and so, in a context of perpetual political exception—a history of the *legitimation* of such practices presents a different trajectory. Notions of a "better shelter" actually emerged in the metropolitan West during World War I, in a context where members of a national community who carried with them some expectation of rights—like citizens of the Austro-Hungarian Empire—were presented with the prospect of model emergency housing at the cost of internment. The subsequent history of the model camp is one in which the substitution of shelter for rights protection was rendered so irreducible, necessary, and well-nigh "normal" that it ceased to be questioned as anything but an advance in humanitarian reason. Pointing toward the history of this substitution, we also point toward a distinction between the currently proliferating empirical histories of the camp, on the one hand, and the history of the camp's legitimization in a global shelter imaginary, on the other.

As the subordination of the refugee to given notions of refuge, the global shelter imaginary has attained normative status at exactly the same moment in history when the premises of detention—the promise of return or resettlement promised in international conventions—have given way to a condition of indefinite temporariness among camp dwellers. And with that crisis in the paradigm, the majority of the world's dispossessed elect to live under the conditions of "pirate urbanism" that have yielded what Mike Davis has termed a "planet of slums."[14] Chapter 3, "'Protection Space,'" traces how the existence of what are termed "urban refugees" has simultaneously challenged and advanced the global shelter imaginary by prompting institutions of humanitarian governance to advance new euphemisms for protection that only serve to extend notions of shelter to wherever the displaced might find themselves. "Protection Space" is the most common of these euphemisms.

If the global shelter imaginary describes a condition under which IKEA's branding of domesticity became the unacknowledged paradigm of rightless relief, the conclusion of this work, "Airbnb Refugee," reviews how euphemisms like "protection space" have permitted the new dwelling models of the global sharing economy to offer themselves as alternatives without real distinctions. Airbnb's actual proposals to promote its platform as a way to host refugees is examined here against the same concept of cosmopolitan right for which it mistakes itself. The right of the stranger to protection is finally incorporated within a rescue fantasy of shelter provision that simply reaffirms the prerogatives of "superhosts" to reject hospitality to whomever they wish whenever they wish.

14. Davis, *Planet of Slums*.

1. Better Shelter / Better Refugee

A Global Shelter Crisis?

The United Nations Refugee Agency (UNHCR) estimates that approximately one out of every ninety-seven people on the planet is now displaced by war, persecution, or catastrophe, with the factors generating this catastrophe showing few signs of abating.[1] As of the end of 2019, 79.5 million people were counted as dispossessed: 45.7 million of them were internally displaced and 33.8 million have sought safety across international borders.[2] Of the latter, only 4.2 million have attained the status of "asylum seekers," even as an additional 10 million humans are now designated as being without nationality or at "risk of statelessness."[3] Only a small percentage of the 100 million people displaced between 2010 and 2019 have been repatriated, in what amounts to a widening tendency toward protracted displacement.

The dispossessed of the present surpass the number of people cast adrift at the end of World War II. The refugees and internally displaced people (IDPs) of 1945 amounted to 7 percent of the global

1. UN High Commissioner for Refugees, *Global Trends: Forced Displacement in 2019*.
2. UN High Commissioner for Refugees, *Global Trends: Forced Displacement in 2018*.
3. UN High Commissioner for Refugees, *Global Trends: Forced Displacement in 2018*.

Figure 2. Innovative refugee shelter changes the lives of thousands of refugees around the world. March 7, 2018. Copyright UNHCR.

population and today's refugees inch towards 0.9 percent.[4] If the current crisis appears to be smaller in proportion, however, this is not solely because of the planet's significant population growth. It is also an effect of the global refugee regime itself. Since the creation of the International Refugee Organization (IRO) in 1944, the establishment of the UNHCR in 1950, and the passage of the 1951 Refugee Convention, states have advanced an international refugee protection regime premised on the universal right to seek asylum,

4. Gatrell, *The Making of the Modern Refugee*, 3.

and—faced with the exigent circumstances of the internally displaced and stateless people—they have also extended the right of protection to categories of the displaced that did not fall under original treaties. At the same time, Western states, in particular, have sought to preempt and delimit the exercise of that right in practice. The refugee has thus been suspended between the aspirations of international human rights norms on one hand and the vicissitudes of domestic immigration policies on the other. States have repeatedly pitted the demands of sovereignty against those of human rights in ways that have increasingly "denaturalized/disqualified" populations otherwise worthy of protection.[5] The result has been a progressive and de facto narrowing of the definition of refugees and their cognates so that the positive duty of states toward the displaced has been obscured in a cognitive and moral order characterized by "data gaps" and "category fetishism."[6]

"Smart" Humanitarianism

The true extent of the crisis facing asylum seekers is obscured by the fact that the physical and procedural barriers to people attempting to claim that status have actually never been higher. Australia's reprehensible practice of intercepting refugee ships and directing them to "detention centers" on the island nation of Nauru and on Papua New Guinea's Manus Island is not an outlier of contemporary refugee policy; it conforms to a general tendency on the part of Western states to subordinate "humanitarian refugee resettlement" obligations to a "criminogenic border policing practices" so that asylum claims can be deferred or preempted to begin with.[7]

5. Hathaway, "The Evolution of Refugee Status in International Law"; Islam and Bhuiyan, *An Introduction to International Refugee Law.*

6. Hammerstadt, "The Securitization of Forced Migration." See also Crawley and Skleparis, "Refugees, Migrants, Neither, Both"; FitzGerald, *Refuge beyond Reach.*

7. Michael Grewcock, "'Our Lives Is in Danger'"; National Immigrant Justice Center, "A Legacy of Injustice."

France, as well as a number of other states, has even resorted to the legal fiction of designating detention centers *within* their sovereign borders as extraterritorial sites. This fiction allows them to abrogate their responsibilities under the 1951 Refugee Convention, which calls upon signatories to process the asylum claims of all those who succeed in reaching their shores.[8]

Two observations follow. First, when the right to refuge is neither abrogated nor effectively implemented, humanitarian government, in Didier Fassin's terms, largely orients itself toward the [impression] management of limbo; it rationalizes perpetual internment under provisional conditions.[9] In that process, the "politics of life and the politics of suffering" coincide with a necessary retreat of the state as signatories to international refugee conventions that regularly sanction the creation of refugee enclaves within their borders. Second, as if by common consent, the sociodicy of the dispossessed ceases to be sustained by nation-states and becomes the concern of intergovernmental actors who manage the permanent

8. "The Convention is both a status and rights-based instrument and is underpinned by a number of fundamental principles, most notably non-discrimination, non-penalization and non-refoulement. Convention provisions, for example, are to be applied without discrimination as to race, religion or country of origin. Developments in international human rights law also reinforce the principle that the Convention be applied without discrimination as to sex, age, disability, sexuality, or other prohibited grounds of discrimination. The Convention further stipulates that, subject to specific exceptions, refugees should not be penalized for their illegal entry or stay. This recognizes that the seeking of asylum can require refugees to breach immigration rules. Prohibited penalties might include being charged with immigration or criminal offences relating to the seeking of asylum, or being arbitrarily detained purely on the basis of seeking asylum. Importantly, the Convention contains various safeguards against the expulsion of refugees." UN High Commissioner for Refugees, *The Refugee Convention, 1951,* "Introductory Note"; UN General Assembly, *Convention Relating to the Status of Refugees*; see also Agier, *Managing the Undesirables.*

9. Fassin, *Humanitarian Reason*, 155: "regulation is paradoxically all the more strict because the European space is also a space of the rule of law—and hence of rights, notably human rights."

impermanence of a global internment regime; and then, by entrepreneurial actors involved in capitalist humanitarian initiatives. Together, these actors advance a coercively depoliticized vision of refuge/relief in a context where no actual right to either is generally respected. This is what is commonly referred to as "smart humanitarianism"—that is, a vision of action premised on the universalizability of "market-led business models" in the world of aid, relief, and development.[10]

Circle of Prosperity

Also known as "capitalist humanitarianism," smart humanitarianism is a species of reasoning that accounts for, *but does not explain,* a remarkable partnership between the UNHCR and the IKEA Foundation. IKEA is the UNHCR's largest private-sector partner (200 million dollars, in cash and in kind, from 2001 to 2013). And yet, according to the UN agency, its relationship with IKEA goes far "beyond philanthropy" to reach a "genuine commitment to innovation."[11]

IKEA's own understanding of that commitment is worth elaborating. Analogizing a relation between cosmopolitan consumers of home furnishings, on the one hand, and humanitarian subjects, on the other, the IKEA Foundation asserts that "design" generates "proper solutions" for refugees.[12] "Proper solutions" are, in turn, defined as approaches remarkably consistent with IKEA's own market strategy: they "reflect IKEA's business philosophy of partnership, long-term focus, cost-consciousness, innovation, creativity, constant improvement, and strong ethical behavior."[13] Finally, the

10. Dale and Kyle, "Smart Humanitarianism," 785.
11. UN High Commissioner for Refugees, "IKEA Foundation."
12. Better Shelter, "Better Shelter Awarded Beazley Design of the Year." In this and other publications on the Better Shelter, the IKEA Foundation refers to the product as "theirs," rather than a product of the Better Shelter nonprofit, which strictly speaking it is.
13. "The Way We Work," IKEA Foundation, accessed November 3,

market strategy itself attains the status of a universal ethic. Seeking to "maximize return on invested capital," IKEA has created a moral template not only for living the good life but also for mitigating unlivable ones. Recalling Adam Smith's "virtuous cycle" while intending to replace the "cycle of poverty," IKEA terms this template the "circle of prosperity."[14] This circle emphasizes something very much like the 'greatest happiness principle' once advanced by the Utilitarian philosopher Jeremy Bentham—but it nowhere refers to rights, human or otherwise.[15]

IKEA's forwarding of domestic furniture as, in effect, a vehicle for achieving the good life signals a historic transition from a postwar Nordic model of social democracy that once allied consumer consumption to collective well-being, to a consumer capitalist association of morality with consumption per se.[16] The original model is premised upon a continuum between the nation-state as "home of the people" (*Folkhemmet* in Swedish), the individual homes of the nation-state's citizenry, and the political subjectivity of citizen-consumers who sacrifice luxury for the shared benefit of social goods. In the words of Swedish national propaganda, "Per Albin (Hansson, former prime minister and national father-figure) built

2019, https://ikeafoundation.org/about/the-way-we-work/. Ingvar Kamprad, founder of IKEA, explicitly drew this connection, writing that, "our goal with the IKEA Foundation is in keeping with exactly what we've always tried to do as a home furnishings company"; see "A Better Everyday Life," IKEA Foundation, accessed May 13, 2020, https://ikeafoundation.org/about/.

14. "Circle of Prosperity," IKEA Foundation, accessed June 7, 2018, https://www.ikeafoundation.org/about-us-ikea-foundation/circle-of-prosperity/. It pays to note that in articulating these features of a "better life," the IKEA Foundation exemplifies the type of "computational empathy" discussed in Dale and Kyle, "Smart Humanitarianism."

15. "We always look to monitor and maximise the return on invested capital and improve the effectiveness and efficiency of our support programmes, *so we can be sure we're doing as much we can for as many people as possible*" (emphasis added), "Funding," IKEA Foundation, accessed May 13, 2020, https://www.ikeafoundation.org/about-us-ikea-foundation/funding/.

16. See Mattsson and Wallenstein, eds., *Swedish Modernism*.

the 'home of the people' and Ingvar Kamprad (IKEA's founder) furnished it."[17] The well-furnished home was, here, a locus for the Nordic welfare state's imagined community of citizen-consumers and their moral behavior. This home not only subtends IKEA's "democratization" of domestic design, but—as we discuss in "A Better Refugee," below—also Nordic architectural phenomenology with its normalizations of "home" and "dwelling" as universal conditions. In this sense, presumably offering an expanded set of domestic conditions to displaced people, the Better Shelter represents a physical universalization of governance through domesticity, even as the political rights that would have made it a "home for the people" are actually withdrawn.

A Better Shelter

The centerpiece of the partnership between the UNHCR and the IKEA Foundation is a "social enterprise" called BetterShelter.org, which produced the packaged emergency dwellings deployed in Burkina Faso. Its mandate is to transform the landscape of camp humanitarianism by building upon IKEA's successes with flat-pack design and packaging technologies to produce a universal and replicable postemergency dwelling. The Better Shelter arrives on site in two boxes that contain pipe frames, connectors, and plasticized insulation panels for the exterior. After an embarrassing false start with sheathing that proved to be highly flammable, version 2.0 now meets SPHERE standards.[18] With the exception of a ground anchoring system that requires the use of tools, each unit is held together with pressure fittings that can be tightened by hand.

BetterShelter.org's own presentation of what it calls "the product" emphasizes its humility. The social enterprise takes pains to acknowledge that the Better Shelter cannot compete with or

17. Quoted in Lindqvist, "The Cultural Archive of the IKEA Store," 57.
18. Sphere Project, *Humanitarian Charter and Minimum Standards in Humanitarian Response*, 239–86.

replace standard tents as emergency housing for the displaced, whether in terms of cost or utility. Nor can the Better Shelter serve the purpose of resettlement, which requires infrastructure, civil and property rights, and architecture. "Our shelter looks like a kid from Sweden drew a house" is how one BetterShelter.org representative describes a product that is purposely designed to have a maximum lifespan of three years.[19] This is because the social enterprise interprets the stark alternative between tents and houses in terms of duration—i.e., along an axis of permanence. In its telling, the Better Shelter is a product designed to respond to protracted refugee conditions by "bridging the gap" between emergencies and so-called durable solutions.[20]

But as it claims to make incremental gains along the axis of durability, the Better Shelter also replicates the same illogic of humanitarian governance it is intended to redress. In the first instance, it is important to note that there have been virtually *no* incremental gains in managing the settlement of forced migration in the past generation. Since the trend line is so entirely in the other direction, incrementalist assumptions about how to offer dwellings with a slightly longer lifespan must be understood as palliatives for an order that is actually characterized by category fetishism and inaction. More to the point, however, the Better Shelter cannot compete with or situate itself within a continuum spanning between tents and houses because the preceding are not indices of duration but rather

19. Terne, "Presentation of the Better Shelter Product."
20. As the founder of BetterShelter.org, Johan Karlsson, put it: "I had thought of humanitarian aid as a temporary measure, something to protect for the short term. But the average time of a refugee situation is almost twenty years. In many of the camps where we are working today refugees have stayed for years and years . . . [the Better Shelter can be] . . . integrated into transitional shelter programs so that you can extend the lifespan and link the emergency aid you are having here to more development aid." Johan Karlsson, "Innovative Design—A Winding Path," Tedx Talk, TEDxNorrköping, December 4, 2017, YouTube video, 18:01, https://www.youtube.com/watch?v=15cJPKKd0i0.

moments in a juridico-political paradox that defines protracted refugee crises to begin with. This is because the dispossessed can neither move on while under the protection of the United Nations nor resettle in durable homes: the only migration available is an intolerable refoulement of endangered populations and the only homes on offer must be temporary shelters to meet the concerns of host states. These states typically tolerate camps only so long as they are provisional structures, no matter how many decades they may remain in place—a condition that was already well understood and anticipated by Palestinians who were forced to erect dwellings *behind* the canvas of tents in Jordanian refugee camps after the 1948 Arab–Israeli war. These Palestinians correctly intuited that the juridico-political status of refugees could not be reconciled with the form of their abode.

The Image of Relief

And yet, the Better Shelter matters: *not because it heralds a significant advance in housing the dispossessed, but because it is credited with doing so.* This crediting demands analysis as a first step in understanding the political logic of which it is a part. The gap between what the Better Shelter can actually do and the privileged position it occupies in the attention economy becomes explicable with reference to the "iconography of predicament" that the Better Shelter advances.[21] As it implicates design in the amelioration of forced migration, the Better Shelter corroborates the humanitarian order's technocratic framing of refugees and their "crisis" to begin with; it becomes, in other words, the image of a humanitarian response to a crisis as it is defined by the present humanitarian order.

No less important than the *image* of relief that the Better Shelter corroborates is the transposition that takes place in the process of formalizing that image. When a 2016 Museum of Modern Art

21. Gatrell, *Making of the Modern Refugee*, 114.

exhibition on habitat insecurity made the Better Shelter model its curatorial "centerpiece"—to cite the museum's director, Glen Lowry—it effectively bandwagoned with IKEA, the Design Museum, and other institutions in a complex process of reputation management.[22] By engaging in an act of patronage toward the Better Shelter, an art institution with a billion-dollar endowment simultaneously engaged in "virtue signaling" in the social sphere—a species of legitimacy swapping that attends efforts to relate design to humanitarian crisis.[23]

These complex processes of swapping social capital cannot be mistaken for simple cases of mutual endorsement. To the contrary, the participants' noticeable acts of mutual distancing enhance their own legitimacy as independent and "disinterested" social actors, even as those same gestures ratify the practical logic that attends all symbolic exchange. This is because "repression" of the exchange and "taboos" concerning any reference to it are the hallmarks of symbolic economies.[24] BetterShelter.org now takes pains to dis-

22.   The Museum of Modern Art, "Preview | Insecurities, and How Should We Live," featuring Glenn Lowry, Sean Anderson, and Juliet Kinchin, The Museum of Modern Art, September 30, 2016, YouTube video, 45:16, https://www.youtube.com/watch?v=kltVGARh7xM. The phenomenon of "bandwagoning" has been analyzed extensively in the field of international relations theory, where it connotes a process of seeking relative safety in numbers. But even there it also implies the meaning attributed to it in the social sphere, where to bandwagon is to adopt "a popular point of view for the primary purpose of recognition and/or acceptance by others" (Urban Dictionary, s.v. "bandwagon," December 17, 2003, accessed July 11, 2018, https://www.urbandictionary.com/define.php?term=bandwagon).

23.   To speak of "virtue signaling" is not to imply that these institutions acted cynically. Rather, it means that their members have a "practical sense" that imbricates them in the ordering of their reality—often, in ways that often involve an "exchange of honor." That practical sense: "operates at a pre-objective, non-thetic level; it expresses this social sensitivity which guides us prior to our positing objects as such." Bourdieu and Wacquant, An Invitation to Reflexive Sociology, 20. On exchanges of honor, see the chapter "The Economy of Symbolic Goods" in Bourdieu, Practical Reason, 92–124.

24.   Bourdieu, Practical Reason, 83–84.

tinguish itself from IKEA, just as MoMA seeks to present the exhibition of the Better Shelter and its corollaries as an act of public education rather than as the endorsement of a particular solution or policy recommendation. "We're not advocates, but we have a voice in the world," states Glenn Lowry when asked what MoMA's role is or should be in the amelioration of forced migration. The more frequently the relation between design and humanitarianism is in this way questioned, the more surely it is legitimated by virtue of the imputed reflexivity of those involved in cementing the connection.[25]

In this way, a sociodicy of relief is advanced in the trafficking of symbolic goods depicting the social good. But so, too, are "unthought categories of thought which delimit the thinkable."[26] The social position occupied by the Better Shelter points to a particular way of understanding a social-political crisis so that it retroactively conforms not only to the way smart humanitarianism frames its objects and problems but also to a broader and unexamined framework of understanding. According to this framework—the global shelter imaginary—"what goes without saying" about the dispossessed presupposes all that "comes without saying" about their relation to architecture.[27]

---

25. Bourdieu, *Practical Reason,* 78. In such denials, Bourdieu argues, there is a "hidden tacit accord": adversaries interested in the same social field "disagree with one another, but they at least agree about the object of disagreement." These generate what Bourdieu calls the "profits" of universalization that attend the language of disinterested and apolitical humanitarianism, which is the language of its protection of humanitarianism as disinterested and apolitical. This is illustrated, in part, in the way that Sean Anderson, the curator of the Habitat insecurity exhibit at MoMA, suggests that "architecture becomes a litmus of the very problem . . . if we propose architecture as a solution it ignores the problem. . . . I come back to the idea that shelter is something we make, but when shelter is imposed . . . that's when the architecture changes . . . and that's when the meaning of architecture begins to reinforce or negate the very idea of humanitarianism." The Museum of Modern Art, "Preview | Insecurities, and How Should We Live."

26. Bourdieu, *Leçon sur la leçon* (Paris: Editions de Minuit, 1982), as cited in Bourdieu and Wacquant, *Invitation to Reflexive Sociology*, 40.

27. Bourdieu, *Outline of a Theory of Practice,* 167.

To invoke a global shelter imaginary, then, is to recall the symbolic work necessary to legitimate and naturalize the relationship between "design thinking" and humanitarianism. This means that the global shelter imaginary refers, first, to the normalization of the *given* compendium of housing solutions for the dispossessed as a response to their political plight. These comprise an array of design prototypes that are regularly circulated and recirculated in mediaspace so that they come to constitute a self-referential and self-evident totality—that is, a universal image of relief. Not only does this composite image of shelter constitute an attempt to capture global displacement as, at once, product placement opportunity, branding possibility, market niche, professional subfield, and raw material for the production of social capital, it also represents what Bourdieu calls an "imposition of forms" whereby appearances become indistinguishable from necessity. In the novel paradigms, projects, and practices that are intended to "respond" to the housing needs of the dispossessed—and in the predominant theorizations of the relation between shelter and dispossession—the global shelter imaginary has come to dominate thinking and acting around dispossession. The global shelter imaginary, that is, perpetuates a particular technocratic pairing of crisis and relief at the expense of any other words one might crib together to analyze the conditions under which refugees are actually forced to negotiate the conditions of their existence, in part as a result of that same pairing.

For these reasons, the global shelter imaginary is a reification of what Saskia Sassen calls a "savage sorting" of humanity.[28] In the identification of dispossession with the problem of shelter, the dispossessed are replaced with their own concept as that concept has been elaborated with increasing success by the stakeholders in a technocratic humanitarian infrastructure. But symbolic work involves not only an "imposition of forms" but also an observance of "formalities": smart humanitarians themselves *accept and advance*

28. Sassen, *Expulsions*, 1.

the unquestioned and unexamined doxa of what James Ferguson has called "the anti-politics machine" to describe the coercive politics of depoliticization by means of which the planet's undesirables are managed.[29] Stated more simply: the global shelter imaginary corroborates a normative characterization of refugees as shelter seekers, transforms them into the subsidiaries of "refuge," and in the process hypostatizes the problem of dispossession into a reprise of what the nineteenth century euphemized as "the housing question." Indeed, one could go further to suggest that as it concerns itself with the morphologies of shelter, humanitarianism forgets its externality to its object and redoubles the displacement of the displaced people it purports to assist.

A Better Refugee

To suggest that the global shelter imaginary turns the world's dispossessed into ancillaries of the forms of rightless relief offered to them is, in the first instance, to say that it aligns with larger tendencies in the management of the world's undesirables. As is the case with other modalities of aid, assistance, and relief, contemporary shelter humanitarianism presumes and demands human types that correspond to the prototype solutions it offers: it relies, for example, on procedures of "participation," "partnership," and "empowerment" to at once map and reconcile the sociopolitical status of the displaced onto paradigms of consumer behavior. In a video released in celebration of World Intellectual Property Day, BetterShelter.org indicated that the social enterprise would "increase its impact . . . by developing its design together with partners and end users."[30]

29. "Depoliticizing everything it touches, everywhere whisking political realities out of sight, all the while performing, almost unnoticed, its own preeminently political operation of expanding bureaucratic state power." Ferguson, *The Anti-Politics Machine,* xiv.

30. Better Shelter, "Better Shelter @ World Intellectual Property Day," May 8, 2017, YouTube video, 2:29, https://www.youtube.com/watch?v=V9xegwnBWVQ.

Here, the dispossessed are solicited to approach aid—and in the process, to redefine themselves—in the same ways as those assisting them participate in their own personal purchasing decisions. In the process, the language of "needs" sublates any talk of rights, just as the act of selecting from given categories of possibility presents itself as the only possible model of agency, a presentation that is as normative as it is oppressive.

More than this, though, the global shelter imaginary is also of a piece with a shift from "the protection of refugee rights to the protection of refugee bodies" and the concomitant subordination of human rights to humanitarianism, in the context of which forms of overt attention given to the displaced actually constitute society's tacit inattention to mass displacement.[31] For example, when U.S. President Donald Trump referred to his country's border with Mexico as the site of a "humanitarian" crisis, he advanced a pattern he did not invent, and brought the United States in closer alignment with the speech acts of European counterparts.[32] As Heller and Pécoud have convincingly shown, in the now-generalized designations of "humanitarian borders," sites of interdiction commonly present themselves as the "sites of saving."[33]

In this unnecessary sacrifice of human rights to humanitarianism and of legal protection to relief, the bodies of the displaced are expected to conform to the norms and qualifications assigned to them. The evidence of this transformation is overdetermined. For example, as Welton-Mitchell had indicated, "medical reports documenting asylum seekers' physical and/or mental health are increasingly being used within Refugee Status Determination (RSD) proceedings as objective evidence to support asylum claims."[34] In

31. Pasquetti, Casati, and Sanyal, "Law and Refugee Crises."

32. Gharib, "Humanitarian Experts Debate Trump's Use of the Term 'Humanitarian Crisis.'"

33. Heller and Pécoud, "Counting Migrants' Deaths at the Border," 10.

34. Welton-Mitchell, "Medical Evidence in Refugee Status Determination."

that same process, Fassin and d'Halluin outline the ways in which "medical authority progressively substitutes itself for the asylum seeker's word," in an act of "objectification" that erases the "experience of the victims as political subjects."[35] Under these conditions, victim testimonies concerning the psychological experience of trauma become, at the same time, testimonies of the coercion whereby a humanitarian order transmutes political grievances into symptoms so that suffering confirms the seeming "apoliticism" of the humanitarian order itself.[36] And in camps, finally, "biometric registration" serves as a passport to both food and shelter relief, even as it creates "digital refugees at risk of new forms of intrusion and insecurity."[37]

Arguably, then, the new humanitarian order is a kind of biopolitics machine—that is, a form of governmentality in which "postsovereign power" coincides with the regulation of the biological life of populations no less than with the ability to discipline individual bodies.[38] As part of this order, the global shelter imaginary produces forms of subjectivity adequate to its own typologies. Not only is the global shelter imaginary the place where all precarious forms of existence are now expected to make themselves at home, it is also "orthopractic" in the sense that what is actually being designed in the process of creating a "better" shelter is a better refugee.[39]

The better refugee is a means to a particular end: the product placement of "humanitarian design." The evidence of such practices is as anecdotal as it is pervasive. Shared with 2.7 million followers, for example, a 2019 UNHCR Tweet featuring weight-loss celebrity and "high profile UNHCR supporter" Jillian Michaels invites viewers to "feel chills" as the reunion of two South Sudanese refugees is filmed

35. Fassin and d'Halluin, "The Truth from the Body," 597. See also Pestre, "Instrumentalizing the Refugee's Body through Evidence."

36. See Keeler, "Peacebuilding."

37. . Jacobsen, "Experimentation in Humanitarian Locations," 144. See also Monk and Herscher, "New Universalism."

38. Muhle, "A Genealogy of Biopolitics," 79.

39. Certeau, *The Practice of Everyday Life*, 147.

against a backdrop of Better Shelters in the Democratic Republic of Congo.[40] But this is just one instance of the way in which the better refugee is called upon to rehearse the mission statements of the venture humanitarians who support them in ever-proliferating press releases, videos, and the "churnalism" that follows them.[41] As far as the Better Shelter–IKEA alliance is concerned, this means that—in media at least—the dispossessed appear to be those "whose lives have been changed" because they have been provided with "a *safer* more *dignified* home away from *home*."[42]

It is difficult to discern if what experimental psychologists call "demand characteristics"—that is, "observer expectancy effects"—among the Better Shelter's representatives or the assumption of "good participant roles" by the dispossessed actually affect or motivate the testimony captured in the calls articulated in Better Shelter media for safety and its fulfillment.[43] What is clear, however, is that the *formal* function of the refugee testimony in IKEA Foundation videos such as "Almost 30,000 Better Shelter Units . . ." is to interpolate between levels of analysis—that is, between in-security in the international arena and domestic safety, or between politics and private life. Refugees become "better" as they fulfill this function. In "Almost 30,000 Better Shelter Units . . ."—the 4:45 minute IKEA Foundation video about Better Shelters on the Greek island of Lesvos—the statements of a Syrian taxi driver and his wife refer primarily to safety as distance from war ("When there are no loud sounds, no planes, no shooting, my kids and I can sleep"). But as

40. UNHCR, the UN Refugee Agency (@refugees), "These friends never thought they'd see each other again. The moment when they reunited will give you chills. #DayofFriendship," Twitter, July 30, 2019, 11:50 a.m., https://twitter.com/refugees/status/1156139872450744320.

41. In this connection, it bears stating that between 2017 and 2019, BetterShelter.org's own mission statement dropped any reference to "persons displaced by conflicts."

42. Better Shelter, "Almost 30,000 Better Shelter Units Improve Refugee Living Conditions around the World."

43. Nichols and Maner, "The Good-Subject Effect."

they also express satisfaction with the lockable door of the Better Shelter they occupy in the Kara Tepe camp, the refugees' statements are edited into a flow of no fewer than fifteen other discrete shots or narration segments that syntagmatically elide locks with security *per se*. In this way, better refugees give stakeholders in Better Shelters an opportunity to introduce and repeat key euphemisms for the *denial* of politics, so that the fulfillment of the implicitly natural and universal need for enclosure, for example, stands in for the security one can only gain when one is ensured the right to have rights: "whether you live in the north, south, wherever. You need a roof over your head and it needs to be safe," states Jonathan Spampinato in affirmation of IKEA's politics of depoliticization of the refugees' political plight.[44]

In the media, repeated references to "privacy" and "dignity" in the provision of shelter stand in for an entirely absent concept of agency, which would be necessary to address the indignity of internment and dispossession. The better refugee doesn't always have to do the heavy lifting of interpolating the loss of political agency into the acquisition of domestic dignity on their own. Sometimes, this acquisition is accomplished textually, by the sequencing of clauses in which a displaced person's acknowledgment of their precarity is completed by a venture humanitarian presentation of temporary shelter as the solution. Take, for example, a 2019 press release describing how an Iraqi man named Jadaan returned to his destroyed village equipped with a Better Shelter: "'There are not many opportunities for us here, but our children have hope for a better future,' said Jadaan, *whose temporary home means being able to return to a sense of dignity* after years of being rootless."[45]

44. "A Better Shelter for Refugees," IKEA Foundation, October 25, 2017, YouTube video, 4:50, https://www.youtube.com/watch?v=0p0TfPIK7_Y.

45. "Iraqi Families Return to Rebuild Their Lives: Better Shelters Offer a Feeling of Home in a City in Ruins," Better Shelter, accessed November 3, 2019, https://BetterShelter.org/iraqi-families-return-to-rebuild-their-lives-better-shelters-offer-a-feeling-of-home-in-a-city-in-ruins/ (emphasis added).

"When Does a Shelter Become a Home?"

In even more common references to the Better Shelter as a "home away from home," the international politics of forcible displacement is transmuted into implicit equivalence with the generic substate problem of homelessness and with the resolution of this problematic in domesticity. Repeating and thereby reinforcing the question asked by the curator of the MoMA "Insecurities" exhibition in IKEA's "Human Shelter" documentary, the author of an "Info-Migrants" feature on design for refugees asks: "When does a shelter become a home?"[46] Two observations follow. First, in historical contrast with the kind of public debates that followed Krystof Wodiczko's Homeless Vehicle project, which proposed *as a form of social criticism* to improve the lives of indigents by making it easier to live on the American street, few seem to ask whether it is actually *possible* or *right* for a shelter to become a home—or even to estrange the implicit necessity of the transposition of shelter to home.[47] Second, as the question of "when is a shelter a home?" reverberates within humanitarian mediaspace, the global shelter imaginary blurs the difference between the rightless condition of the refugee and the socioeconomic displacement of the homeless within the domain of formal, or at least nominal, rights inside of one's own country.

The question "when is a shelter a home?" is posed in ways that imply the answer offered in advance by a BetterShelter.org press release entitled: *A Home Away from Home.*[48] Organized as a direct address to the reader, who is in turn put in the position of a forcibly displaced person—"You have had to leave your own home, your routines and your everyday life behind. Now, all around are 25,000 other people just like you"—the pamphlet hypostatizes mass displacement into the experience of an imputed Better Refugee capable

46. MacGregor, "Design for Refugees."
47. Hebdidge, "The Machine Is Unheimlich."
48. Better Shelter, *A Home Away from Home.*

of rationalizing self-interest along a prescribed path leading to the Better Shelter. In the process of "impersonation," as Quintilian defined this figure of thought, the reader-as-Better Refugee is defined as someone who recognizes the "simple fact of having a home, a right so fundamental most of us take it for granted, can dramatically improve the physical and psychological situation of refugees. . . . [and that the] . . . Better Shelter meets the basic needs for the activities of basic living, for privacy, security and familiarity."[49] Invoking needs as rights in this fashion, the coercive politics of humanitarian apoliticism here recruits an entirely abstract Better Refugee into the affirmation of rightless relief.[50]

It bears stating that the implicit exchange of the right to have rights for the gratification of human needs—protection for relief—is only effected in the reported "sense" of shelter. For example, the Better Refugee's conscripted testimonials about the feeling of privacy offered by the Better Shelter actually hinge on product claims that, for example, the shadows cast behind plastic walls are invisible from without.[51] Similarly, the reported "sense" of security is premised on the existence of lockable door to a structure that only offers what one of the Better Shelter's designers calls "a semi-rigid feeling" of polyolefin panels that can be cut into pieces with a good knife. And the Better Shelter's "sense" of being a "home away from home" rests on the feeling that it feels "a bit more secure" than a tent.[52]

This emphasis on "feeling" is not incidental. It is part of the phenomenological disposition of the propaganda of rightless relief, which appeals to the belief that human experience of that world is

49. Better Shelter, *Home Away from Home.*

50. "Temporary Homes for 4000 Iraqis," Better Shelter, accessed November 3, 2019, https://BetterShelter.org/temporary-homes-for-4-000 -iraqis/; Hunt Institute, "OXHIP 2015: Profile of Better Shelter, Inventive Housing for Refugees," October 12, 2015, YouTube video produced by The Kelley Group, 2:30, https://www.youtube.com/watch?v=fmk9yemxfQo.

51. "Revisiting Lesvos," Better Shelter, accessed November 3, 2019, https://BetterShelter.org/revisiting-lesvos/.

52. "Revisiting Lesvos," Better Shelter.

universal and beyond politics. It is precisely this "jargon of authenticity," as Theodor Adorno termed it, that permits humanitarian government to speak for universal humanity, and for its unwitting apologists to invoke the writings of Martin Heidegger (specifically, "Poetically Man Dwells") when promoting a documentary about "human shelter" sponsored by IKEA itself.[53] Here, the human senses become plenipotentiaries for the *common*-sense politics actually abandoned to the global shelter imaginary.

The phenomenological disposition that is so useful to such appeals to universal humanity has a deep connection with the architectural culture that generated the Better Shelter. As post–World War II architects in Europe and the United States became aware of the way in which their labor was unequally distributed in a world of decolonization and postcolonial conflict and violence, interwar phenomenology was brought to bear on the experience of architecture so as to render this awareness irrelevant. Architects derived from the thinking of Martin Heidegger that the experience of "dwelling" was not contoured by nationality, race, gender, class, sexuality, or any other social category but rather was "the free sphere that safeguards each thing in its essence"—this from Heidegger's essay "Building Dwelling Thinking," translated into English in 1971 and widely read in schools of architecture in the following decades.[54] For Heidegger, then, homelessness was not unequally borne by the wretched of the earth but rather an existential condition shared by all "mortals" that could be resolved by "thinking":

> What if man's homelessness consisted in this, that man still does not even think of the proper plight of dwelling as the plight? Yet as soon

53. Adorno, *The Jargon of Authenticity*; Nikolaj Fremming, "Screening of The Human Shelter Documentary Film," June 1, 2018, Vimeo video, 04:14, https://vimeo.com/273032055; in a gender-inclusive amendment to Heidegger's text, at the end of the screening, IKEA head of design, Marcus Egman and the film director, Boris Bertram, concur that "poetically humans dwell on this earth."

54. See Heidegger, "Building Dwelling Thinking," in *Poetry, Language, Thought,* 351.

as man gives thought to his homelessness it is a misery no longer. Rightly considered and kept well in mind, it is the sole summons that calls mortals into their dwelling.[55]

It is not at all accidental that a phenomenologically inflected universalization of architectural experience has been consolidated, reified, and advanced, from the 1950s to the present, by Scandinavian architects and designers. In the first instance, the "conspicuous modesty" of Swedish postwar design coincided with a model of social democracy premised in part on citizens' rights to access quality housing, consumer goods, and domestic furnishings.[56] This association of a phenomeology of dwelling with a kind of design universalism was subsequently advanced, from the 1970s to the present, by Scandinavian architects like Christian Norberg-Schulz and Juhani Pallasmaa and Swiss architects like Peter Zumthor—each architects living, working, and teaching among the primary beneficiaries of global class apartheid.[57] When the humanitarian promoters of the Better Shelter echo Heidegger in making claims for "poetic dwelling," then, two phenomenologically inspired universalizations intersect with and augment one another, yielding a philosophical legitimization for the global shelter imaginary's biopolitical project.

In the fabrication of Better Refugees/Shelter Seekers, however, the global shelter imaginary reveals more than the biopolitical core of humanitarian government and its attendant claims to reason. As the global shelter imaginary invokes a phenomenology and poetics of "dwelling" unthinkingly drawn from the thinking of actual Nazis, it advances biopolitics in claims for something resembling its supersession. Here, the biopolitical regulation of life

55. Heidegger, *Poetry, Language, Thought*, 363.
56. Daloz, "Political Elites and Conspicuous Modesty"; Mattsson and Wallenstein, *Swedish Modernism*; Murphy, *Swedish Design*.
57. Norberg-Schulz, *Existence, Space & Architecture*; Christian Norberg-Schulz, *Genius Loci*; Peter Zumthor, *Thinking Architecture*; Pallasmaa, *The Thinking Hand* and *The Eyes of the Skin*.

presumes itself to advance an ideal beyond politics by appealing to the dignity of unqualified existence. And this is how the global shelter imaginary confuses bare life with cosmopolitan right and the state of exception with the common good. This, finally, is how a life horrifically suspended between the "fact and law," to cite Giorgio Agamben, is postured into a regulative ideal.[58]

---

58. Agamben, *The Omnibus Homo Sacer,* 141.

2. There Has Always Been a Better Shelter

Once they had left their homeland they remained homeless, once they had left their state they became stateless; once they had been deprived of their human rights they were rightless, the scum of the earth.

—HANNAH ARENDT, *Origins of Totalitarianism*

Rightless Relief

The global shelter imaginary provides a symbolic—and symbolically effective—resolution to the political paradox presented to sovereign states by the presence of people who cannot be naturalized as citizens of those states, repatriated to the states they have left, or permitted to move on. These are dispossessed people whose dispossession is at once marked and obscured by their categorization as "refugees" or victims of forced migration—which is to say as people taking refuge and assigned "notional" rights as such.[1] To categorize the *dispossessed* as *refugees,* that is, is to gesture toward forms of refuge indistinguishable from indefinite interment and to do so while there are increasingly fewer instances when states provide the dispossessed any refuge at all.

Deployed to ostensibly "protect" refugees, camps have thereby come to function as displacements of political questions about the sovereignty of the state presented by refugees seeking asylum into architectural questions about shelter. In so doing, the mandate to "protect" refugees manifests as enhancements of refugee assistance

1. Oliver, *Carceral Humanitarianism.*

Figure 3. "New type of housing barrack," Refugee Camp in Wagna, Austria, around 1918. Image from Hartwig Fischel, "Bauanlagen der staatlichen Flucht-lingsfürsorge," *Der Architekt* 21 (1916/1918): 20.

and little more. Humanitarianism's exchange of rights—the human rights only available to citizens of states—for rightless relief is thereby rendered as a provision of homes to the supposedly homeless.

This exchange is a part of a history of projects to resolve the paradox that the dispossessed present to sovereign states in a bio-politics—a politics of managing life without rights. This history was already becoming visible to Hannah Arendt in the years after World War II. Writing in 1951, in "The Decline of the Nation-State and the End of the Rights of Man," Arendt pointed to the status of the camp as the "practical substitute" for the refugee's "nonexistent homeland":

All discussions about the refugee problems revolved around this one question: How can the refugee be made deportable again? The second World War and the DP camps were not necessary to show that the only practical substitute for a nonexistent homeland was an internment camp. Indeed, as early as the thirties this was the only "country" the world had to offer the stateless.[2]

2. See the chapter "The Decline of the Nation-State and the End of the Rights of Man" in Arendt, *Origins of Totalitarianism*, 284.

Arendt wrote the preceding in the form of a critique. Six decades later, the *same* country of encampment she referred to does not solicit critique as much as promotional literature, professional carpetbagging, philanthro-capitalism, and churnalism: within the global archipelago of spaces where the dispossessed are contained and managed, a global shelter imaginary idealizes the country and condition of encampment, and the bare life that takes place there, as a moral territory in which capital and professional expertise are redistributed to the supposed benefit of the new wretched of the earth. This global shelter imaginary has thereby transformed encampment from what Arendt, in the years just after World War II, called "practical"—an *ad hoc* attempt to manage the human remainder resulting from the state's paradoxical relationship to the stateless—into a regulative ideal, a normative and potentially perfectible condition. In so doing, the "right to shelter" that underscores this imaginary has become compensation for, rather than complementary to, rights accorded to humans and citizens alike: the rightless people that Arendt termed "the scum of the earth" are precisely those people whose right to shelter is asserted, defended, and advanced in the contemporary global shelter imaginary as a plenipotentiary for the legal/political rights actually denied them.[3]

Since the turn of the twentieth century, stateless people and people displaced by war and other crises from states to which they cannot return have each been categorized as "refugees." Arendt, however, insisted on a distinction between these two categories of people, arguing that the condition of statelessness, exacerbated by the dissolution of the Austro-Hungarian, Ottoman, and Russian Empires after World War I, was "the newest mass phenomenon in contemporary history" and stateless people (the "*apatrides*") were "the most symptomatic group in contemporary politics."[4]

3. Arendt may have borrowed the term "scum of the earth" from Arthur Koestler's 1941 memoir, *Scum of the Earth,* about his detention at Camp Le Vernet in France the previous year.
4. Arendt, *Origins of Totalitarianism,* 277.

The global shelter imaginary is structured by the particular relationship that obtains between statelessness, on the one hand, and encampment, on the other: the "shelter" provided by encampment absorbs the stateless in a form that is valorized as moral rather than analyzed as biopolitical. This valorization poses moralized encampment as an improvement or even solution to biopolitical encampment. The history of the camp, however, is a history in which moralized encampment has *always* functioned as a displacement and tacit legitimization of encampment's biopolitical status. This history was inaugurated with refugee camps at the end of the nineteenth century and first decades of the twentieth century; while camps in European colonies took form as a species of militarized internment, camps in wartime Europe took form in a wide variety of ways, including in some cases camps posed as spaces of moralized domesticity. As the camp continued to develop through the twentieth century, the colonial laboratory of internment was conjoined to—and perhaps superseded by—a metropolitan laboratory of legitimizing internment, the latter yielding an imaginary of rightless relief in which *shelter* is always *better shelter*. This imaginary, whose latest manifestation is the Better Shelter, divides the history of the camp as a particular kind of space from a history of the camp's legitimization, normalization, and valorization as a vehicle of rightless relief.[5]

And yet, it is precisely the distinction between these histories and the colonial and metropolitan forms of internment that sub-

---

5. Our argument also supplements the history of the intertwined relationship between counterinsurgency and domesticity laid out by Patricia Owens. Owens explores investments in "improving" or "reforming" the social life of dominated people—the way in which "civilizing missions involve the domestication of dominated others"; in colonial contexts, she locates these investments outside camps and after periods of manifest terror and violence. We point to another intersection of domestication and domination that, in Europe, originated not beyond the camp but within it. See Owens, *Economy of Force*.

tend them that has been blurred in received histories of the camp.[6] In particular, animated by attempts to "globalize" the history of the camp, received histories obscure crucial distinctions between refugee camps emerging from the juridico-political conditions of colonialism and humanitarianism. Blurring these two conditions, globalizations of the camp's history have pointed to morphological contiguities between colonial-era camps in Cuba, India, South Africa, and Latin America and subsequent refugee, internment, concentration, and extermination camps in Europe—relationships premised on carceral enclosure, the barrack as a building type, castramented plans, and other formal features.[7]

Running across two distinctively different juridico-political conditions, these morphological relationships turn away from the crisis of statelessness as the crisis of state sovereignty posited by Arendt and subsequently Giorgio Agamben toward an acceptance and valorization of that crisis in biopolitical form.[8] The predominant morphological understanding of the camp, then, can itself be historicized—a historicization that poses the "globalization" and "commonality" of the camp's history as itself a product, rather than critique, of the morphological turn.[9]

Encampment and the Housing Question

As it emerged in late nineteenth- and early twentieth-century colonial contexts, the refugee camp was described and designed in military terms as a species of campsite or bivouac for armed

6. See, for example, Forth, *Barbed-Wire Imperialism*; Pitzer, *One Long Night*; Nemser, *Infrastructures of Race*; and Stone, *Concentration Camps*.

7. For a sophisticated architectural version of this morphological history, see Grancy, "Die Baracke als architektonische Kippfigur," https://vimeo.com/156405263.

8. On the relationship between globalized histories, humanitarianism, and encampment, see Monk and Herscher, "New Universalism."

9. A paradigmatic example of this morphological turn may be found in Katz, "The Common Camp."

forces.[10] As such, the camp mediated the status of the territory it emerged in as governed by the laws of war rather than the state's rule of law. The first camps posed for people explicitly categorized as "refugees," for example, began to be constructed in 1899 by the British military in South Africa for Boers and indigenous Africans. These were people who were displaced from their homes by the scorched-earth counterinsurgency policy carried out by British forces in response to Boer insurgency campaigns; they were placed in camps that, according to the British, conformed to the stipulated policy of "internment" in the recently framed Hague Conventions.[11]

Originally termed "concentration camps" with reference to the *concentración* of Cuban civilians in fortified or fenced-in towns and villages by Spanish forces during the Cuban War of Independence (1895–98) and Filipino civilians in camps by U.S. forces during their brutal counterinsurgency campaign against Filipino guerrillas (1900–1902), these South African camps were renamed "burgher camps" and "refugee camps" when they began to pass on to civilian administration in 1901. But the castramentation of the camp plan, use of bell or private's tents for shelter, and management of Boer refugees as civilian prisoners of war persisted through the demilitarization of Boer refugee camp administration, each testifying to the militarization of the camp itself.[12]

Received histories of the camp also tend to move from these South African examples to camps in Europe built during the First World War. And yet, as it emerged in European contexts during the First World War, the refugee camp was at times described and

10. See Forth, *Barbed-Wire Imperialism*, 43–128.

11. See Raath and Strydom, "The Hague Conventions and the Anglo-Boer War." According to the 1899 Hague Convention, "Prisoners of war may be interned in a town, fortress, camp, or any other locality, and bound not to go beyond certain fixed limit."

12. See Thomson, *The Transvaal Burgher Camps, South Africa,* posed by its author as the world's first manual on designing and managing the refugee camp. On castramentation as an ideal, see Monk, "The Art of Castramentation."

designed in domestic terms, transfiguring a space of internment into a response to what was widely known in the nineteenth and twentieth centuries as "the housing question."[13] While these camps are outliers in received camp histories, they initiate the genealogy that leads to the Better Shelter and its proliferating equivalents. In this genealogy, the Better Shelter does not merely represent an attempt to improve refugee shelter, as its authors pose it. Rather, as architectural signifiers of domesticity came to function as substitutes for and displacements of lost or expected rights, this genealogy tracks a sequence of "better" refugee shelters and "better" refugee camps for the making of "better refugees": a sequence that, wholly absent in colonial contexts, includes the Better Shelter as one of its most recent instances.

And so, even as almost all World War I–era camps were castramented, as most of them utilized barracks, and as some of them even occupied unused military facilities, some European refugee camps were rationalized as a species of housing. In and after the First World War, this rationalization prompted European states to approach the refugee camp as a figurative or actual contribution to municipal or national housing stocks: components, that is, of existing domestic infrastructures that framed the permanent temporariness of people impossible to assimilate or resettle in architectural terms of permanence. Here, "housing" represented the form in which the idealization of internment took place—an idealization fully lacking in internment's colonial antecedents. In those colonial antecedents, states were contending with people displaced from their homelands. In Europe during and after the First World War, by contrast, states began to contend with people from what Arendt

13. See Herscher, *Displacements*, 102–6. Exploring colonial contexts, Patricia Owens sees housing questions emerging *after* the internment of populations; in the Philippines, for example, she writes that "the forcible removal and concentration of populations was followed by 'policies of attraction,' reform of labor, education, health, and sanitation . . . a form of domestic engineering especially responsive to housewifery." See Owens, *Economy of Force*, 22.

so aptly termed "nonexistent homelands"; as "housing," the camp emerged as an architectural technology to manage this task and, most profoundly, to manage this task's impossibility.

Camps in Europe that appear as outliers, if they appear at all, in received camp histories are therefore central in the development of this architectural technology. In the First World War, several of these seemingly exceptional camps were constructed by the Austro-Hungarian state for "refugees"—a name that primarily referred to members of minority communities that Austro-Hungarian forces forcibly evacuated from the empire's war-threatened eastern provinces.[14] For example, the "garden city" camp in Oberhollabrunn, where barracks were arrayed picturesquely along the topographical lines of a steep hillside, was built for Ruthenian, Romanian, and Polish refugees evacuated from war zones, and the model camp at Gmünd, which included masonry "villa barracks," each with its own garden, was built for Ruthenian, Croatian, and Slovene refugees.[15] These, along with other examples of refugee camps designed according to contemporaneous housing models, testify emphatically to the imaginary of the camp as a form of housing.[16] It is crucial to note that the audience for the camp-as-housing paradigm was not those who inhabited the camps; in these camps, "the average refugee was treated more like a prisoner than a citizen of the monarchy."[17] Rather, the audience was the society that established camps as legitimate spaces to in-

14. See Hermann, "Cities of Barracks." On the legal status of citizens of the Austro-Hungarian empire, see Hirschhausen, "From Imperial Inclusion to National Exclusion."

15. Hermann, "Cities of Barracks," 139.

16. On these camps, see Schwarz, "Architekt Heymann, Ingenieur Gröger und das k. k. Flüchtlingslager Oberhollabrunn"; Schmoll, "Das Flüchtlingslager in Gmünd"; Antje Senarclens de Grancy, *Ein Flüchtlingslager in der Südsteiermark*, project description, n.d., https://iam.tugraz.at/akk/.

17. Hermann, "Cities of Barracks," 135.

tern the refugee *qua* prisoner; modeled as housing, the camp could be assimilated as a non-exceptional space of exception.

In "The Decline of the Nation-State and the End of the Rights of Man," Arendt described the context within which the camp's legitimizing function developed: the years leading up to World War II when European states realized, with shock, "that it was impossible to get rid of [the refugees (repatriation)] or transform them into nationals of the country of refuge [naturalization]."[18] In World War II, she contended, the problem of statelessness was discursively eliminated, and thereby actually consolidated, by inventing the term "displaced persons" to categorize both stateless people and people displaced from states.[19]

The imaginary of camp-as-housing continued to develop in World War II, at least in those places where the legitimization of internment remained salient. In Vichy France, for example, camps were built to intern Roma and other "nomads," following a precedent established in Nazi-occupied France; these camps included Camp de Saliers, which was designed to look like a French village so as to supposedly facilitate the assimilation of Roma—many of them citizens of France—into sedentary French society.[20] That this assimilation never took place—the Roma were deported from Saliers, just as they were from other internment camps—does not represent the deception or contradiction of Saliers's design but rather its function: to legitimize internment, whether it was terminal or concluded by deportation.

The global shelter imaginary that unfolded after World War II in the context of institutionalized humanitarianism consolidated the exchange of rightless relief for rights. This consolidation was animated by and accompanied the reorientation of humanitarianism away from temporary emergency responses toward long-term

18. Arendt, *Origins of Totalitarianism*, 281.

19. Arendt, 279.

20. On the camp at Saliers, see Pernot, *Un camp pour les bohémiens*, and Marie-Christine Hubert, "The Internment of Gypsies in France."

development processes—a reorientation that yielded what Michael Barnett has called "the age of neo-humanitarianism."[21] As Barnett and others have described, this reorientation normalized an evacuation of refugee rights; in the form of an emerging global shelter imaginary, it also normalized the domestication of the refugee camp.

Perhaps most prominent in the framing of this domestication was the work of architect Ian Davis and humanitarian Fred Cuny, within which the camp's relation to housing became crucial to the designation of "successful" camp design.[22] For Davis, the camp's received morphology should be avoided in favor of those drawn from local housing configurations; for Cuny, the camp "should be considered with the same detail as a master plan for a town."[23] Both ambitions yielded an equivocation between camp and housing and new circuits of knowledge exchange between the study of vernacular housing and self-housing in the Global South, on the one hand, and the proposition of shelter for refugees and other dispossessed people, on the other.[24] The *political* problem faced by stateless people—the problem of having no space within which they were endowed with rights, either to stay or to go—was thereby assimilated into the *architectural* problems faced by inadequately housed and unhoused people of all kinds, from the homeless, through slum dwellers, to survivors of disasters and communities displaced from their homes by violence.

In 1980s and '90s, the institutionalization of discourse on the shelter of displaced people formalized a global shelter imaginary;

21. Barnett, *Empire of Humanity*, 97–160.

22. Cuny, "Refugee Camps and Camp Planning"; Davis, *Shelter after Disaster*; Davis, ed., *Disasters and the Small Dwelling*; Office of the United Nations Disaster Relief Co-ordinator, *Shelter after Disaster*; and Cuny, *Disasters and Development*. On this discourse, see Anooradha I. Siddiqi, "Architecture Culture, Humanitarian Expertise."

23. Cuny, "Refugee Camps and Camp Planning," 127.

24. For example, the work of John Turner on self-settlement and self-housing in the Global South would become important for Davis and Cuny: see Siddiqi, "Architecture Culture, Humanitarian Expertise," 376.

this imaginary was, in a sense, the first-order product of standards and practices established for the settlement of the displaced. Key moments in this institutionalization include the 1982 publication of the *UNHCR Handbook for Emergencies,* which included a section on shelter issues; the UNHCR's 1993 First International Workshop on Improved Shelter Response and Environment for Refugees; the 1995 publication of "Shelter Provision and Settlement Policies for Refugees," prepared by Roger Zetter for the 1993 workshop; and the 1996 initiation of the Sphere Project, which intended to "produce globally applicable minimum standards for humanitarian response services."[25] On their own terms, these actions were part of the necessary project to, in the words of the UNHCR, "answer people's urgent need for protection and humanitarian assistance anywhere in the world . . . ensure that refugees at risk have received legal and physical protection . . . [and] develop the mechanisms to reinforce a quick, agile and flexible emergency response capacity"; by 2007, the UNHCR posed itself as able to manage unexpected refugee crises "involving up to 500,000 people," across the globe.[26] And yet, at the same time, these actions also began to normalize the political status of shelter as rightless relief.

Zetter's comprehensive review of refugee shelter practices began with the seemingly indisputable claim that "durable shelter . . . constitutes one of the basic needs for refugees"; "no different from other communities," he continued, "refugee housing represents a cultural commodity; it supports a diversity of functional requirements; it is an important economic multiplier."[27] And yet, elided in this equivocation between refugees and others, which would subse-

25. UN High Commissioner for Refugees, *Handbook for Emergencies*; Zetter, "Shelter Provision and Settlement Policies for Refugees"; Sphere Project, *Humanitarian Charter and Minimum Standards in Disaster Response.* See also Siddiqi, "Architecture Culture, Humanitarian Expertise" 378–81.

26. UN High Commissioner for Refugees, *Handbook for Emergencies,* vii.

27. Zetter, "Shelter Provision and Settlement Policies," 30, 37.

quently be appropriated by IKEA and a host of other humanitarian entrepreneurs, is the particular rightlessness of the stateless. In Zetter's focus on refugee housing, that is, the political rightlessness of the stateless is displaced by a posited right to shelter that is "no different from other communities." And it bears stating that all of this is happening during the "decade of repatriation," when the UNHCR actively participated in the coerced return or resettlement of refugee populations.

Zetter wrote in full awareness of the ways in which "contradictions between the physical permanency of housing, shelter production processes and the presumed temporariness of refugees . . . penetrate to the heart of the dilemmas of refugee policy making and assistance."[28] For him, however, camps and other enduring forms of refugee shelter present "a direct physical challenge to the . . . presumed temporariness of refugees."[29] What may be a "physical challenge" to this temporariness, however, is also the physical form in which temporariness is made to indeterminately persist but also, and still more, in which this persistence is transformed from an exigency into a regulative ideal in the shape of Better Shelters and their analogues.

And so, in the two decades since the publication of Zetter's review of refugee shelter practices, those practices have become the object of steadily increasing attention and investment, each facilitated by the corporatization of humanitarianism in the wake of the 1999 declaration by the United Nations and global business leaders of a "global compact" to "harness the energy and influence of multinational corporations to act as good corporate citizens."[30]

28. Zetter, "Shelter Provision and Settlement Policies," 33.
29. Zetter, "Shelter Provision and Settlement Policies," 47.
30. UN Secretary-General, "Secretary-General Proposes Global Compact on Human Rights, Labour, Environment, in Address to World Economic Forum in Davos."

Camp Humanitarianism

The Better Shelter is but one particularly well-known and celebrated product of the many produced through this alliance between multinational corporations and humanitarian institutions; it is also a metonym of a camp humanitarianism that, repeatedly subjecting itself to "lessons learned" and continually orienting itself around "best practices," substitutes attention to a purported refugee *housing question* for attention to the *politics of displacement* that yield refugees and other dispossessed people in the first place.

> The Better Shelter meets the needs for the activities of basic living, for privacy, security and familiarity. It is a safe base offering a sense of peace, identity and dignity. And though it may be humble, it is somewhere even the most vulnerable people on earth can call a home away from home.[31]

This copy, from BetterShelter.org's publicity material, takes the substitution of homelessness for dispossession to perhaps its most extreme point: the equivalence of rightless relief in the form of a Better Shelter in a refugee camp to the home, of whatever sort, inhabited by a citizen of a nation-state endowed with the expectation of rights as such. The conditions of domesticity that this copy points to—privacy, security, familiarity—along with domesticity's supposed emotional consequences—peace, identity, dignity—are here reduced to products of a kit of parts: locking doors, operable windows, opaque (actually "non-transparent") walls, and so on. Rendered as such, domesticity becomes not only autonomous and self-explanatory but also totalizing and all-encompassing: when you "have" a "home," you not only have all that you need now but also all that you ever had. The political conditions of displacement, along with the political conditions that displacement eliminates, disappear in the form of a home exchange. And the growing number of displaced people who reside in urban areas rather than

31. Better Shelter, *Home Away from Home*, 3.

camps—now estimated at 60 percent of the world's population of the displaced—also disappear; the Better Shelter not only substitutes homelessness for dispossession, but also substitutes shelter, better or otherwise, for the planet of slums that actually shelters the world's dispossessed.

3. "Protection Space"

HAVING REACHED A MOMENT in human history when a strategic partnership in impression management between UNHCR and IKEA has successfully subordinated the brute fact of mass dispossession to the architectural image of its alleviation, it would seem that a global shelter imaginary now holds sway. Within the attention economies of refugee suffering, the given solution—a flat-pack IKEA dwelling—now represents the problem of forced migration so completely that the majority of the world's displaced are disappeared in the representation of their plight. Within the given logic of the global shelter imaginary, the provision of humanitarian relief either disqualifies the dispossessed from consideration as humanitarian subjects worthy of political rights or, worse, recruits them into a new, specifically urban paradigm of protection that is functionally indistinct from abandonment.

The global shelter imaginary takes two principal forms. First, it presents itself to view in the idealization of camp humanitarianism itself. Framed as an improved post-emergency dwelling, the Better Shelter of the UNHCR/IKEA partnership facilitates the perpetuation of what scholars of critical humanitarianism have called a "camp bias," at exactly the moment in history when the majority of refugees (many of whom were born and matured in camps) have decided to abandon lives under a permanent state of exception and to take their chances in environments where the UN offers

Figure 4. "Makeshift Houses," in Peri-Urban Refugee Settlement erected with the assistance of the UNHCR's Global Distribution Tool (GDT). December 12, 2019. Copyright UNHCR

no prospect of or appeal to protection.[1] Second, the global shelter imaginary introduces itself to view in the way that the UN has subsequently euphemized that same *lack* of protection as the inverse: a fictive "protection space" that extends humanitarian governance into what Mike Davis has termed a "planet of slums"—that is, the condition of privatized squatting under which the majority of the world's urban precariat now live.[2]

"Compulsory Voluntary Repatriation"

The relation between the Better Shelter of a declining but normative camp humanitarianism and the "protection space" nominally

1. Edwards, "'Legitimate' Protection Spaces."
2. "Pirate urbanization is, in effect, the privatization of squatting." Davis, *Planet of Slums,* 40.

extended to the growing urban refugee population is not merely paradigmatic; it is historical. These two articles of contemporary humanitarian doxa—the Better Shelter and the "protection space"—began to complement one another and, in the process, complete the global shelter imaginary in the context of a crisis of classification that took place in 2005. Then, a group of Sudanese migrants who had been denied refugee status by UNHCR in Cairo decided to build their own refugee camp directly in front of the agency's offices to protest their relegation to what Pascale Ghazaleh has called a "closed file limbo."[3] For more than three months, approximately two thousand people self-interned in their own refugee camp in Mustapha Mahmoud Park and organized their lives through committees tasked with maintaining the community. This, so that they might better appeal and protest the manner in which their asylum claims had been adjudicated by the UN. (Numbers varied from 1,500 to 2,500 souls.)

The Sudanese protesters' claims against UNHCR may well have been motivated by self-interest, but they also exposed the workings of a geopolitics of abandonment that goes against the agency's mandate. In the course of its efforts to assist populations trapped "between sovereigns"—that is, between the will of states that generate or receive the dispossessed—UNHCR has been repeatedly forced to erode the first of its mandated functions, namely international protection of rights, and compromise on the second, which requires it to offer assistance leading to "durable solutions."[4] Unable to challenge state parties to meet their own obligations pertaining to the legal protection/asylum of refugees, the agency has sought to fill the gap and, over time, also found itself the world's chief "administrator of misery."[5] It is a government of limbo for those

3. Ghazaleh, "In 'Closed File' Limbo"; Kagan, "Assessment of Refugee Status Determination Procedure at UNHCR's Cairo Office 2001–2002."

4. Haddad, *Refugee in International Society*.

5. UN High Commissioner for Refugees [Luise Druke], *Mobilizing for Refugee Protection*.

who cannot resolve their asylum status but who also cannot move on. Where the "search for durable solutions" once referred to the "repatriation, integration, or resettlement" of the dispossessed, it is now a term of art that refers to humanitarian governance of those for whom the right to protection/asylum is increasingly a fiction, even for the UN.

The Sudanese asylum seekers' key demand was that UNHCR resume the practice of conducting individual refugee status determination interviews (RSDs). In June 2004, UNHCR suspended such interviews and "automatically provided all applicants with yellow asylum seeker cards, which offer temporary protection against refoulement."[6] The agency seemingly took this step in response to an announced ceasefire between the government of Sudan and the Sudan People's Liberation Army. But in doing so, UNHCR in Cairo weakened core protections of the 1951 refugee convention, which calls for the adjudication of asylum claims on an individual basis.[7] (This statute was pushed for by Western powers, who feared the possibility that asylum could be granted *en masse*.) But, conversely, it also protects asylum seekers from exclusion as members of a group.[8] The Sudanese protesters correctly understood the agency's action as both a weakening of the protection mandate and a prelude to what it itself termed "compulsory voluntary repatriation"[9]—i.e., the pressuring of yellow or "red" cardholders who had already been denied asylum to return to Sudan on the grounds that the conditions that were, or would have been, the basis for their asylum claims no longer obtained and that therefore their status no longer required a review.

Their fears were not unfounded. In the decade following the fall of the Soviet Union, the UN effectively relaxed the standards of

6. Azzam, ed., *A Tragedy of Failures and False Expectations,* 8
7. On the "individualist" approach to refugee management, see Hathaway, *The Law of Refugee Status,* 2–5. For a comprehensive explanation of the RSD process and its implications for the fate of asylum seekers in that period, see "UNHCR's RSD Policy: Quick Guide."
8. Loescher et al., eds., *Protracted Refugee Situations,* 12.
9. Azzam, *Tragedy of Failures and False Expectations,* 36.

protection for repatriating populations and "developed terminology and concepts such as 'safe return,' which stipulated that conditions in the home country did not have to improve 'substantially' but only 'appreciably'" in order for the UN—and not the dispossessed—to determine what might reasonably qualify as "voluntary repatriation."[10] As Gil Loescher explains, in the course of this "decade of repatriation," the distinction between voluntary repatriation and refoulement was blurred, and UNHCR even participated in acts of forced migration.[11] (The UN would eventually facilitate the repatriation of over 300,000 refugees to South Sudan, despite continuing insecurity and conflict there.) The key point here is not only that these actions resulted in mass suffering (or that the UN eroded the voluntary character of repatriation under rewordings such as "safe return"), but that in the course of doing so, UNHCR established a precedent for *euphemizing* abandonment-as-protection that would prove relevant to the emergence of a global shelter imaginary.

For its part, UNHCR's Cairo office repeatedly disqualified the protesters' standing as persons of concern to UNHCR, even as the spectacle of a self-built refugee camp in the heart of Cairo may have forced the agency to enter into negotiations with them. (UNHCR's first response was to close its offices.)[12] In a press release issued on October 30, UNHCR sought to invalidate the protesters' requests—

10. Loescher et al., eds., *Protracted Refugee Situations,* 51.

11. Loescher, Betts, and Milner, eds., *The United Nations High Commissioner for Refugees (UNHCR),* 48.

12. These responses accord with the attitudes laid out in UNHCR's 1997 urban refugee documents: "irregular movers are often among the most vehement of protesters, although rejected cases, those refused assistance, as well as the psychologically disturbed might all, at times, prove violent and dangerous to themselves and staff . . . UNHCR staff should not hesitate to seek the intervention of local authorities against refugees or asylum-seekers who break national laws. Experience has shown that clear messages, such as closing down the Branch Office and calling in the local police at the beginning of a violent protest, is the most effective way in bringing it to an early and peaceful close." UN High Commissioner for Refugees, *UNHCR Comprehensive Policy on Refugees in Urban Areas.*

which, again, foregrounded concerns about refoulement by other names, and for that reason petitioned the resumption of the RSD process—and advanced two related arguments. The first was that the protesters were, for the most part, not refugees but economic migrants from southern Sudan "who fell outside the agency's mandate" and had thus been accorded "closed file" status. The second was that the signing of the peace agreement "increased nexus requirements for status recognition and created *new opportunities for protection* in Sudan, so that UNHCR's responsibility to refugees from that area changed."[13]

None of this was true, as a report on the protests by the Forced Migration and Refugee Studies [FMRS] program of the American University in Cairo makes clear. The demonstrators were from all parts of Sudan, and a survey of the park population undertaken in December 2005 showed that "43 percent had yellow asylum seeker cards and 24 percent had blue recognized refugee cards" that gave them refugee status.[14] The majority of these souls were or should have been "persons of concern" to UNHCR, while the remainder may have been victims of various forms of category fetishism.[15] Negotiations continued, and—following the intervention of a delegation from UNHCR's headquarters in Geneva in November—a tentative agreement was reached on December 17. The UN would reopen the RSD process and include "closed files" but, citing security concerns, stipulated that individual protesters could not return to the park after their cases had been reviewed. In a challenge to the remarkable and sustained display of solidarity practiced by the Sudanese protesters, UNHCR effectively presented them with a variation of the "prisoners' dilemma" in which collective action and self-interest were to be treated as irreconcilable alternatives. No one defected. The protesters accepted the agreement but refused to abandon the park until *all* cases had been reviewed. On

13. Azzam, *Tragedy of Failures and False Expectations,* 37.
14. Azzam, 38.
15. Ghazaleh, "In 'Closed File' Limbo," 25.

December 22, UNHCR communicated with the Egyptian Ministry of Foreign Affairs and indicated that "it could do no more," thereby paving the way for the forced evacuation of the protesters.[16] On the evening of December 29, approximately four thousand riot police surrounded the park, attacked the population, and killed at least twenty-eight protesters; approximately half of those killed were children, many of whom were trampled to death. The survivors were sent to Egyptian detention centers. "It is extremely sad that people had to die," stated Astrid Van Gerderen Stort, spokeswoman for the UNHCR in Cairo.[17]

"Irregular Movers"

In both its attitude toward the Sudanese asylum seekers and in its strategy toward their three months of protest, UNHCR's Cairo office had either adopted or coincidentally reproduced the commonplace attitudes of UNHCR's institutional culture laid out in a controversial 1997 policy document concerning urban refugees.[18] Largely identifying urban refugees with "irregular movers" who leave a country of first asylum for the purpose of "assistance shopping" in another, the 1997 *UNHCR Comprehensive Policy on Urban Refugees* sought to disaggregate opportunistic migrants from the ranks of those who might be legitimate persons of interest to the agency, and to disincentivize the behavior of what it considered professional refugees seeking further assistance in place or resettlement in third countries.[19]

16. Azzam, *Tragedy of Failures and False Expectations,* 66.
17. Curtis, "Refugees Die in Police Raid."
18. Whitaker, "20 Killed as Egyptian Police Evict Sudanese Protesters"; actually UNHCR both affirmed and denied that it had asked the Egyptian government to intervene. UNHCR in Cairo also stated that it was "very shocked and saddened" by what had taken place. See Azzam, *Tragedy of Failures and False Expectations,* 13–14.
19. UN High Commissioner for Refugees, *UNHCR Comprehensive Policy on Refugees in Urban Areas.*

The events in Cairo in 2005 would be credited, in part, with triggering a comprehensive reconsideration of UNHCR's "restrictive urban refugee policy" and with the subsequent release of a new policy document in 2009. Reviewing the "negative generalizations" of the 1997 policy paper as artifacts of an institutionalized bias that favored, "unjustly, the individual treatment of urban cases compared to those in rural settlements and camps," the new document suggests that the former policy's concern with assistance mining coincided with the agency's *lack of concern* with its own obligations under the protection mandate.[20] To rectify this, "the 2009 document used the notion of 'protection space' as its organizing principle":

> When refugees take up residence in an urban area, whether or not this is approved by the authorities, UNHCR's primary object will be to preserve and expand the amount of *protection space* available to them.[21]

Something is wrong here, and it bears some elaboration if one hopes to understand the proper relation between the concept of "protection space" and the extension of a global shelter imaginary. Jeff Crisp, the author of the 2009 policy revision concerning urban refugees, is correct to foreground the institutionalized biases and bigotry evident in the earlier policy document. (It is impossible to overlook the fact that the *UNHCR Comprehensive Policy on Urban Refugees* suggested that some national groups were, by virtue of their "nomadic traditions" or histories of "economically driven migration," more prone to engage in forms of "irregular movement.")[22] But in fact, one of the principal concerns of the repudiated 1997 urban refugee policy document was the *erosion* of the protection

20. UN High Commissioner for Refugees, *UNHCR Comprehensive Policy on Refugees in Urban Areas,* 94.

21. Crisp, "Finding Space for Protection," 94.

22. Nor can one fail to notice that the report characterized political protest among "irregular movers" as pathology. UN High Commissioner for Refugees, *UNHCR Comprehensive Policy on Refugees in Urban Areas,* 4.

mandate posed by an assistance paradox—a game of chicken—into which UNHCR had been forced by host states in their dealings with urban refugees.[23] Both the 1997 document and the 1995 *Policy and Practice Regarding Urban Refugees* that informed it are, in part, responses to a condition in which some states had shifted eligibility determination (protection) onto UNHCR and then ceded responsibility for assistance in the process. The result, they argued, was that the agency "sometimes falls into a trap of providing assistance year after year in order to buy, and retain, asylum."[24] The flawed and biased reports of the 1990s were clearly misguided in thinking that UNHCR should begin to deny assistance to urban refugees under some circumstances. But it is also clear that their authors feared the creation of a condition in which assistance could become *a substitute for protection.*[25]

On the face of it, the term "protection space" merely seems to refer to the location where the UN's protection mandate and the host state's protection obligation/responsibility overlap and are in force, either by mutual consent or tacit agreement. There, asylum seekers and refugees exist in a legal zone "free from persecution and from which they will not be returned to a territory where life or freedom would be threatened."[26] In context, "protection space" also implies an *extension* of that zone to places beyond camps—which are, historically, the normative abodes of protection itself—in order to address a perceived protection "gap" among the dispossessed. Nothing could be further from the truth: as various scholars of international refugee law have shown, there are originary differences in the definition of the term "protection" as it appears in the governing

23. Note that Crisp highlights that the 1997 report had no separate section on protection, and that it was overly concerned with assistance to the undeserving. See Crisp, "Finding Space for Protection," 94.

24. UN High Commissioner for Refugees, *UNHCR's Policy and Practice Regarding Urban Refugees, a Discussion Paper,* 14.

25. UN High Commissioner for Refugees, *UNHCR's Policy and Practice Regarding Urban Refugees,* 7.

26. Dallal Stevens, "What Do We Mean by Protection?" 237.

legal instruments, and these have generated vigorous debates concerning its meaning and import.[27] Is protection to be understood in terms of surrogacy—that is, as the extension of responsibilities abrogated by the state? Or does it demand, prima facie, a broader conception of the term that extends beyond the fulfillment of a legal and political obligation to ensure the rights of the dispossessed? On the one hand, UNHCR has answered the question in the affirmative. On the other, the perceived need to expand the given definition of protection has resulted in what Stevens has, somewhat skeptically, described as a "protection industry" whose product/principal commodity is a package of neologisms for rights and obligations that no intergovernmental body can actually deliver or guarantee:

> the literature abounds with new concepts—"temporary protection," "surrogate protection," "complementary protection," "humanitarian protection," "protection space"—which sit alongside the old of "international protection" and "diplomatic protection."[28]

The "language of protection" cannot be disambiguated. On the other hand, its official genealogy begins to lay bare the problem that the perceived need for a term like "protection space" exhumes but cannot resolve. A UNHCR Policy Development and Evaluation Services (PDES) report that served as a basis for the urban refugee policy document of 2009 rehearses a bifurcation of mandates that was repeatedly enacted by subsequent claims for "protection space" over the course of the term's career. In it, "protection space" refers, first, to an "expanded notion of surrogacy" that encompasses "all activities through which the rights of refugees and asylum seekers are ensured."[29] A conceptual shift follows: adopting the logic of an Inter-Agency Standing Committee [IASC]

27. See Goodwin-Gill, "The Language of Protection"; Fortin, "The Meaning of 'Protection' in the Refugee Definition"; and Stevens, "What Do We Mean by Protection?"

28. Stevens, "What Do We Mean by Protection?" 244.

29. Barnes, *Realizing Protection Space for Iraqi Refugees,* 5–7; see also UN High Commissioner for Refugees, *Note on International Protection.*

model referred to as "the egg," the expanded space of protection is no longer to be identified solely with the state and (the sites of) its obligations to the dispossessed—typically, camps—but with refugees and the rights they carry with them in a deterritorialized albumen of international protection.

But the PDES report also introduces a second meaning/origin/etymology contrary to the first: "in countries sensitive to being seen as countries of asylum, *protection space is used as a euphemism for 'asylum space.'*"[30] As a semantic artifact of deference to sovereigns, the term "protection space" refers to a zone of coaxed state obligations to protection rather than to a given "egg" of rights. In a syntagmatic fashion, the report then links "protection space" with the concept of "humanitarian space" (itself a correlate of the "humanitarian operating environment") to describe what is, in the final analysis, a *space of assistance* necessary to secure protections that are revealed to be as *aspirational* by the second definition as they are treated as complete in the first.[31]

To be clear, the extension of protection implied by a deterritorialized concept of "protection space" is at the same time its revocation. That logical contrariety—irreducible because it describes the constitutive contradiction between the positive sovereignty of states and the negative sovereignty of the international system—is here simultaneously acknowledged and disavowed. Better Shelter's advocates treat the state of permanent impermanence—between impossible "resettlement" and unthinkable "refoulement"—in exactly the same way: as a mere sequencing problem. To the degree that the PDES document defines "protection space as an environment which enables the delivery of protection activities and with which the prospect of providing protection is optimized,"[32] it splits the difference between the human "right to have rights" and the

30. Barnes, *Realizing Protection Space for Iraqi Refugees,* 11. Emphasis added.
31. Barnes, *Realizing Protection Space for Iraqi Refugees,* 11.
32. Barnes, *Realizing Protection Space for Iraqi Refugees,* 12.

state's role as their guarantor into a single fantasy—in the complex psychological framing of the term—that is both "anticipatory and retroactive."[33] Protection space becomes the imagined form of assistance necessary to realize the same protection space as a *given* zone of rights.

Abandonment as Hospitality

From the standpoint of the global shelter imaginary—from the standpoint of the humanitarian order's subordination of the refugee to the *given* notion of refuge—the question here is not what protection space fails to deliver to the dispossessed but rather what work it does for the current humanitarian order. What does the elimination of protection under the sign/image of its universal extension actually potentiate? We are offered, after all, a kind of politics in which human beings are imagined to be surrounded by a bubble of rights/protection they can take with them anywhere, in a context where the most minimal protections once offered on condition of humanitarian internment are themselves rendered precarious.

Indeed, this *inverse* relationship between claims for a new, extensible, and universal image of protection, on the one hand, and the abandonment of the protection mandate, on the other, points toward a provisional answer. This is that UNHCR's regular acknowledgments that protection space and its "sister concept," humanitarian space, are always "shrinking" seem to coincide with—and *motivate*—further expansions of the protection space argument. For example, the public statements of Erika Feller—who was UNHCR'S Assistant High Commissioner for Protection in the years following the adoption of the 2009 urban refugee policy—refer to protection space in relation to a degraded "asylum architecture." This even as she continued to normalize the concept. The more Feller spoke of protection space, the more protection became something notional, and

33. Gallop, *Reading Lacan,* 81.

the more she indicated that there was "less room to act," the more that acting—in the sense of a dramaturgical response—became a normative response.[34]

And that is the point. This triumph of a notion of protection indistinct from assistance—or more properly, the success of a syntagmatic substitution whereby assistance presents itself as a surrogate for surrogate rights—is co-constitutive with transformations in the global shelter imaginary. If the Better Shelter partnership between the world's largest provider of home furnishings (IKEA) and the planet's biggest refugee landlord (UNHCR) brilliantly instituted architecture as a plenipotentiary for the valorization of rightless relief, then protection space—which aimed to contend with the planet's urban refugees—introduced itself as both a crisis and a market opportunity in the further "imagineering" of assistance-as-protection.

34. Kelly Oliver makes a similar point in her brilliant study *Carceral Humanitarianism*; see also UN High Commissioner for Refugees, *Statement by Erika Feller, Assistant High Commissioner—Protection, UNHCR, at the "Refugee Futures" Conference.*

Conclusion: Airbnb Refugee

Refugees moving to a new city face many challenges. Though
many of them have the support of a caseworker, stable housing
can be hard to come by. Having free, temporary housing gives
them peace-of-mind while they start their new life. Your home
could help someone get settled into their new community.

—*"Host Newcomers Who Are Moving to Your City." Airbnb Open
Homes, https://www.airbnb.com/openhomes/refugee-housing.
Accessed February 29, 2020.*

THE TRIUMPH of the global shelter imaginary now rests on in its
near transparency. The successful subordination of the refugee to
the given image of refugee has presupposed the liberalization of
"Better Shelters" and "protection spaces" to such an extent that
these concepts no longer carry the institutional burdens associated
with their original names. The proliferation of "Better Shelters" has
gone hand-in-hand with their disappearance as such. The plasticized structures no longer carry their original name, except in the
social-media posts of their inventors. More commonly, they are now
designated as RHUs (short for Refugee Housing Units, in UN par-
lance) even as their function as postemergency dwellings regularly
competes with and gives way to demand for the flat-pack huts to
serve as offices, clinics, and pandemic-era quarantine structures.[1]

1. See UNHCR, the UN Refugee Agency (@refugees), "Screws bolts
panels These recently assembled Refugee Housing Units will provide
safe and dignified spaces to undertake medical screenings in quarantine
centres in order to identify people in need of protection. via @recere,"

Figure 5. "Airbnb 'Open Homes' Refugee Housing." https://www.airbnb.com /openhomes/refugee-housing. Accessed October 28, 2020.

Having represented the substitution of protection with relief so successfully, the Better Shelter is no longer tasked exclusively with the branding of refugee domesticity as a surrogate for rights.[2]

"Protection Space" always implied the extension of the same tacit swap of relief for rights to any location on the planet. Conceived of as a way to acknowledge and at the same time contain the challenges to camp humanitarianism posed by the existence of a growing number of "urban refugees," protection space has, like the Better Shelter, given way to the forms of its generalization. The IASC's "egg model" off assistance-cum-protection has been superseded by any equally fantastic paradigm developed by the hospitality industry: the Airbnb refugee.

Twitter, July 15, 2020, 12:47 a.m., https://twitter.com/Refugees/status /1283171198126493698.

2. Jeff Crisp (@JFCrisp), "Are UNHCR staff now under instructions to talk about 'displaced people' rather than 'refugees'? That's what it's beginning to look like . . . ," Twitter, August 7, 2020, 5:10 p.m., https://twitter.com /JFCrisp/status/1291753628265570304.

"Open Homes" and the Closure of Refugee Rights

Offering its hosts an opportunity to accommodate refugees as well as paying customers, Airbnb launched its "Open Homes" program in February 2017—about a year after the launch of the Better Shelter. According to Airbnb cofounder Joe Gebbia, "In the past, it was really difficult for people to open up their home to someone in need"; Open Homes allows Airbnb hosts to offer their rooms for free to asylum seekers and refugees—or, more precisely, to organizations taking charge of their welfare—and therefore make it easier for homeowners to contribute to accommodating the displaced.[3] Referring to the global "refugee crisis" that reached a peak in the summer of 2017, Gebbia claimed that, "now leveraging Airbnb's core competency is easy for anyone who has a spare room or apartment and wants to connect with relief organizations and play a small role in tackling this global challenge."[4]

The "people in times of need" that Open Homes proposes to support are categorized as "evacuees, relief workers, medical patients and their caregivers, refugees, and asylum seekers."[5] This list symptomatizes the practical, political, and ideological labor of the global shelter imaginary; including refugees and asylum seekers among diverse other groups with housing needs, their legal status and rights are replaced by a generic status of homelessness. The substitution of rightless relief for rights is here at once rehearsed and expanded: with the advent of Open Homes, now "the public" is able to augment the state in the provision of this relief.

This substitution marks the liberation of the paradigm of abandonment as assistance from the camp and its global deployment in

3. Rima S. Aouf, "Airbnb Launches Open Homes Refugee Housing Platform."

4. Aouf, "Airbnb Launches Open Homes."

5. "Who Is Eligible to Book on Open Homes?" Airbnb Help Center, accessed August 7, 2020, https://www.airbnb.com/help/article/2597/who -is-eligible-to-book-on-open-homes-as-a-guest.

the fiction of its liberalization—i.e. that this assistance can now be provided without state guarantors of protection because "protection space" itself migrates. And yet, even as the introduction of rightless refugee relief to the putative sharing economy presents itself as a triumph of moral action—an opportunity for compassionate individuals to assist suffering others—it furthers the transformation of refugee protection from a right that states are obligated to respect into a privilege that is provided according to the racialized and gendered economy of supply and demand.

On the one hand, the Open Homes platform takes care to inform refugees, asylum seekers, and their legal hosts that

> Guests using Open Homes for Refugee or Asylum Seeker housing can only book through a trusted nonprofit partner. All guests must have the legal status of a recognized refugee entitled to international protection as determined by the UNHCR and/or have begun the process of seeking asylum in the country where they currently reside.[6]

And yet, on the other hand, the rights of refugees and asylum seekers as guaranteed by the 1951 Refugee Convention and other international agreements are ignored in favor of the putative capacity of the housing market to accommodate them.[7] With the advent of Airbnb's Open Homes program, then, the fate of refugees with re-

6. "Who Is Eligible to Book on Open Homes?" Airbnb Help Center.

7. Article 21 of the 1951 Refugee Convention stipulates that "Contracting States . . . shall accord to refugees lawfully staying in their territory treatment as favorable as possible and, in any event, not less favorable than that accorded to aliens generally in the same circumstances," UN General Assembly, *Convention Relating to the Status of Refugees*. In addition, Article 43 of the International Convention on the Protection of the Rights of All Migrant Workers and Members of their Families stipulates that "Migrant workers shall enjoy equality of treatment with nationals of the State of employment in relation to . . . access to housing, including social housing schemes, and protection against exploitation in respect of rents," UN General Assembly, *International Convention on the Protection of the Rights of All Migrant Workers and Members of Their Families*. On the right to shelter, see UN Office of the High Commissioner for Human Rights, *Fact Sheet No. 21, The Human Right to Adequate Housing*.

spect to accommodation now can rest on being chosen as a "guest" by an Airbnb host. (What appears as a blessing is yet another hurdle). "Everyday @airbnb hosts are welcoming strangers into their homes and building bridges between cultures and communities . . . We must stand with refugees and do our part to promote belonging for ALL people."[8] This tweet from Joe Gebbia, on the occasion of 2018's World Refugee Day, eloquently speaks to the moralized closure of refugee politics advanced by Airbnb's Open Homes program.

Between IKEA's Better Shelter, on the one hand, and Airbnb's Open Homes, on the other, the claim of the refugee on political understanding and cognition is, for all intents and purposes, dissipated. What remains, instead, is a *sociodicy* of relief in which the humanitarian order confuses itself for its object. This is how, finally, the contemporary history of refuge is marked by what Jacques Derrida called "an always possible perversion of the law of hospitality" into its contrary: the abrogation of cosmopolitan right.[9]

8. Joe Gebbia (@jgebbia), Twitter, June 20, 2018, 4:21 p.m., https://twitter.com/jgebbia/status/1009441195502682113.

9. See the essay "On Cosmopolitanism" in Derrida, *On Cosmopolitanism and Forgiveness*, 17.

Bibliography

UN Documents and Reports

Barnes, Anne E. *Realizing Protection Space for Iraqi Refugees: UNHCR in Syria, Jordan, and Lebanon.* New Issues in Refugee Research, Research Paper No. 167. UNHCR. January 24, 2009. https://www.refworld.org /docid/4c2325700.html.

Office of the United Nations Disaster Relief Co-ordinator. *Shelter after Disaster: Guidelines for Assistance.* New York: United Nations, 1982.

UN General Assembly. *Convention Relating to the Status of Refugees.* July 28, 1951, United Nations, Treaty Series, vol. 189, 137. https://www .refworld.org/docid/3be01b964.html.

UN General Assembly. *International Convention on the Protection of the Rights of All Migrant Workers and Members of Their Families: Resolution / Adopted by the General Assembly.* December 18, 1990 (A/ RES/45/158). https://www.refworld.org/docid/3b00f2391c.html.

UN High Commissioner for Refugees (UNHCR) [Romain Desclous]. "Conflict, Violence in Burkina Faso Displaces Nearly Half a Million People." UNHCR. October 2019. https://www.unhcr.org/news/briefing /2019/10/5da03eee4/conflict-violence-burkina-faso-displaces-nearly -half-million-people.html.

UN High Commissioner for Refugees (UNHCR) [Luise Drüke]. *Mobilizing for Refugee Protection: Reflections on the 60th Anniversary of UNHCR and the 1951 Refugee Convention.* New Issues in Refugee Research, Research Paper No. 227. UNHCR. December 2011. https://www .refworld.org/docid/4f38d71e2.html.

———. "IKEA Foundation." UNHCR. https://www.unhcr.org/ikea -foundation.html.

———. "The Global Compact on Refugees." UNHCR. 2018. https://www .unhcr.org/the-global-compact-on-refugees.html.

———. *Global Trends: Forced Displacement in 2018.* UNHCR. June 20, 2019. https://www.unhcr.org/5d08d7ee7.pdf.

——. *Global Trends: Forced Displacement in 2019*. UNHCR. June 18, 2020. https://www.unhcr.org/5ee200e37.pdf.

——. *Handbook for Emergencies*. Geneva: United Nations, 1982.

——. "IKEA Foundation." UNHCR. https://www.unhcr.org/ikea -foundation.html.

——. *Note on International Protection*, July 7, 2000 (A/AC.96/930). https:// www.refworld.org/docid/3ae68d6c4.html.

——. *The Refugee Convention, 1951: The Travaux Préparatoires Analysed with a Commentary by Dr. Paul Weis*. UNHCR. 1990. https://www .refworld.org/docid/53e1dd114.html.

——. *Statement by Erika Feller, Assistant High Commissioner—Protection, UNHCR, at the "Refugee Futures" Conference, Monash University Prato Centre, Italy, 11 September 11, 2009*. September 11, 2009. https://www .refworld.org/docid/4ad5a1202.html.

——. *UNHCR Comprehensive Policy on Refugees in Urban Areas*. UNHCR. March 25, 1997. https://www.refworld.org/docid/41626fb64.html.

——. *UNHCR's Policy and Practice Regarding Urban Refugees, a Discussion Paper*. UNHCR Inspection and Evaluation Service. October 1, 1995. https://www.unhcr.org/research/evalreports /3bd4254e7/unhcrs-policy-practice-regarding-urban-refugees -discussion-paper.html.

UN Office of the High Commissioner for Human Rights (OHCHR). *Fact Sheet No. 21, The Human Right to Adequate Housing*. Fact Sheet No. 21/Rev.1. November 2009. https://www.refworld.org/docid /479477400.html.

UN Secretary-General. "Secretary-General Proposes Global Compact on Human Rights, Labor, Environment, in Address to World Economic Forum in Davos." Meetings Coverage and Press Releases. Press Release SG/SM/6881. UNSG. February 1, 1999. https://www.un.org /press/en/1999/19990201.sgsm6881.html.

Secondary Sources

Adorno, Theodor W. *The Jargon of Authenticity*. Evanston, Ill.: Northwestern University Press, 1973.

——. *Minima Moralia: Reflections on a Damaged Life*. Trans. E. F. N. Jephcott. London: NLB, 1978.

Agamben, Giorgio. *The Omnibus Homo Sacer*. Stanford, Calif.: Stanford University Press, 2017.

Agier, Michel. *Managing the Undesirables: Refugee Camps and Humanitarian Government*. Cambridge: Polity, 2011.

Arendt, Hannah. *The Origins of Totalitarianism*. 1951; repr., New York: Schocken Books, 2004.

Aouf, Rima S. "Airbnb Launches Open Homes Refugee Housing Platform."
    Dezeen, June 9, 2017. https://www.dezeen.com/2017/06/09/airbnb
    -launches-open-homes-refugee-housing-platform-technology-design
    -news/.

Azzam, Fateh, ed. *A Tragedy of Failures and False Expectations: Report
    on the Events Surrounding the Three-Month Sit-In and Forced Removal
    of Sudanese Refugees in Cairo, September–December 2005.* Cairo:
    American University in Cairo, 2006. http://schools.aucegypt.edu
    /GAPP/cmrs/reports/Documents/Report_Edited_v.pdf.

Barnett, Michael N. *Empire of Humanity: A History of Humanitarianism.*
    Ithaca, N.Y.: Cornell University Press, 2011.

Berlant, Lauren, and Michael Warner. "Sex in Public." *Critical Inquiry* 24,
    no. 2 (Winter 1998): 547–66. https://doi.org/10.1086/448884.

Better Shelter. "Almost 30,000 Better Shelter Units Improve Refugee
    Living Conditions around the World." Press release. *My News Desk,*
    March 28, 2019. http://www.mynewsdesk.com/se/better-shelter
    /pressreleases/almost-30000-better-shelter-units-improve-refugee
    -living-conditions-around-the-world-2852779.

———. "Better Shelter Awarded Beazley Design of the Year," https://
    BetterShelter.org/better-shelter-awarded-beazley-design-of-the-year/.

———. *A Home Away from Home.* December 2015. http://www.BetterShelter
    .org/wp-content/uploads/2015/12/About_Better-Shelter.pdf.

Bourdieu, Pierre. *On the State: Lectures at the Collège De France, 1989–1992.*
    Ed. Patrick Champagne, Remi Lenoir, Frank Poupeau, and Marie-
    Christine Rivière. Trans. David Fernbach. Oxford: Polity Press, 2014.

———. *Outline of a Theory of Practice.* Trans. Richard Nice. Cambridge:
    Cambridge University Press, 1977.

———. *Practical Reason: On the Theory of Action.* Cambridge: Polity Press, 1998.

Bourdieu, Pierre, and Loïc J. Wacquant. *An Invitation to Reflexive
    Sociology.* Chicago: University of Chicago Press, 1992.

Certeau, Michel de. *The Practice of Everyday Life.* Trans. Steven Rendall.
    Berkeley: University of California Press, 1984.

Crawley, Heaven, and Dimitris Skleparis. "Refugees, Migrants, Neither,
    Both: Categorical Fetishism and the Politics of Bounding in Europe's
    'Migration Crisis.'" *Journal of Ethnic and Migration Studies* 44, no. 1
    (2018): 48–64. https://doi.org/10.1080/1369183X.2017.1348224.

Crisp, Jeff. "Finding Space for Protection: An Inside Account of the
    Evolution of UNHCR's Urban Refugee Policy." *Refuge* 33, no. 1 (March
    2017): 87–96. https://doi.org/10.25071/1920-7336.40451.

Cuny, Frederick C. *Disasters and Development.* New York: Oxford
    University Press, 1983.

———. "Refugee Camps and Camp Planning: The State of the
    Art." *Disaster* 1, no. 2 (1977): 125–43. https://doi.org/10.1177
    %2F0896920516640041.

Curtis, Ben. "Refugees Die in Police Raid." *Sunday Telegraph,* January 1, 2006, 29.

Dale, John, and David Kyle. "Smart Humanitarianism: Re-imagining Human Rights in the Age of Enterprise." *Critical Sociology* 42, no. 6 (September 2016): 783–97. https://doi.org/10.1177/0896920516640041.

Daloz, Jean-Pascal. "Political Elites and Conspicuous Modesty: Norway, Sweden, Finland in Comparative Perspective." In *Comparative Studies of Social and Political Elites,* ed. Fredrik Engelstad and Trygve Gulbrandsen, 171–210. Bingley, U.K.: Emerald Group Publishing Limited, 2006. https://doi.org/10.1016/S0195-6310(06)23008-4.

Davis, Ian, ed. *Disasters and the Small Dwelling.* Oxford: Pergamon, 1981.

———. *Shelter after Disaster.* Oxford: Oxford Polytechnic Press, 1978.

Davis, Mike. *Planet of Slums.* London: Verso, 2006.

Derrida, Jacques. *On Cosmopolitanism and Forgiveness.* Trans. Mark Dooley and Michael Hughes. London: Routledge, 2001.

Edwards, Alice. "'Legitimate' Protection Spaces: UNHCR's 2009 Urban Refugee Policy." *Forced Migration Review* 34 (February 2010): 48–49. https://www.fmreview.org/sites/fmr/files/FMRdownloads/en/urban-displacement/edwards.pdf.

Fassin, Didier. *Humanitarian Reason: A Moral History of the Present.* Berkeley: University of California Press, 2012.

Fassin, Didier, and Estelle d'Halluin. "The Truth from the Body: Medical Certificates as Ultimate Evidence for Asylum Seekers." *American Anthropologist* 107, no. 4 (2005): 597–608. http://www.jstor.org/stable/3567378.

Ferguson, James. *The Anti-Politics Machine: Development, Depoliticization, and Bureaucratic Power in Lesotho.* Cambridge: Cambridge University Press, 1990.

FitzGerald, David S. *Refuge beyond Reach: How Rich Democracies Repel Asylum Seekers.* New York: Oxford University Press, 2019.

Forth, Aidan. *Barbed-Wire Imperialism: Britain's Empire of Camps, 1876–1903.* Oakland: University of California Press, 2017.

Fortin, Antonio. "The Meaning of 'Protection' in the Refugee Definition." *International Journal of Refugee Law* 12, no. 4 (October 2000): 548–76. https://doi.org/10.1093/ijrl/12.4.548.

Gallop, Jane. *Reading Lacan.* Ithaca, N.Y.: Cornell University Press, 1985.

Gatrell, Peter. *The Making of the Modern Refugee.* Oxford: Oxford University Press, 2013.

Gharib, Malika. "Humanitarian Experts Debate Trump's Use of the Term 'Humanitarian Crisis.'" *NPR Goats and Soda,* January 9, 2019. https://www.npr.org/sections/goatsandsoda/2019/01/09/683533895/humanitarian-experts-debate-trumps-use-of-the-term-humanitarian-crisis.

Ghazaleh, Pascale. "In 'Closed File' Limbo: Displaced Sudanese in a Cairo Slum." *Forced Migration Review* 16 (January 2003): 24–26. https://

www.fmreview.org/sites/fmr/files/FMRdownloads/en/african
-displacement/ghazaleh.pdf.

Goodwin-Gill, Guy S. "The Language of Protection." *International Journal of Refugee Law* 1, no. 1 (1989): 6–19.

Grancy, Antje Senarclens de. "Die Baracke als architektonische Kippfigur." Lecture at University of Innsbruck symposium "Innovation in Tradition," November 12–13, 2015. Vimeo video by architekturtheorie.eu, February 23, 2016, 59:32. https://vimeo.com/156405263.

Grewcock, Michael. "'Our Lives Is in Danger': Manus Island and the End of Asylum." *Race & Class* 59, no. 2 (October 2017): 70–89. https://doi.org/10.1177/0306396817717860.

Haddad, Emma. *The Refugee in International Society: Between Sovereigns.* Cambridge: Cambridge University Press, 2008.

Hammerstadt, Anne. "The Securitization of Forced Migration." In *The Oxford Handbook of Refugee and Forced Migration Studies,* ed. Elena Fiddian-Qasmiyeh, Gil Loescher, Katy Long, and Nando Sigona, 265–77. Oxford: Oxford University Press, 2014.

Hathaway, James C. "The Evolution of Refugee Status in International Law: 1920–1950." *International and Comparative Law Quarterly* 33, no. 2 (1984): 348–80. https://doi.org/10.1093/iclqaj/33.2.348.

———. *The Law of Refugee Status.* Toronto: Butterworths Canada, 1991.

Hebdidge, Dick. "The Machine Is Unheimlich: Krzysztof Wodiczko's Homeless Vehicle Project." *Walker Art,* August 30, 2012. https://walkerart.org/magazine/krzysztof-wodiczkos-homeless-vehicle-project.

Heidegger, Martin. *Poetry, Language, Thought.* Trans. Albert Hofstadter. New York: Harper and Row, 1971.

Heller, Charles, and Antoine Pécoud. "Counting Migrants' Deaths at the Border: From Civil Society Counter-Statistics to (Inter)Governmental Recuperation." IMI Working Paper Series 143, January 2018. Amsterdam: IMI and AISSR, 2018.

Herscher, Andrew. *Displacements: Architecture and Refugee.* Berlin: Sternberg, 2017.

Hermann, Martina. "'Cities of Barracks': Refugees in the Austrian Part of the Habsburg Empire during the First World War." In *Europe on the Move: Refugees in the Era of the Great War,* ed. Peter Gatrell and Liubov Zhvanko. Manchester: Manchester University Press, 2017. https://doi.org/10.7765/9781526105998.00013.

Hirschhausen, Ulrike von. "From Imperial Inclusion to National Exclusion: Citizenship in the Habsburg Monarchy and in Austria 1867–1923." *European Review of History: Revue Européenne d'histoire* 16, no. 4 (August 2009): 551–73. https://doi.org/10.1080/13507480903063860.

Hubert, Marie-Christine. "The Internment of Gypsies in France." In *In the Shadow of the Swastika: The Gypsies during the Second World War*, vol. 2, ed. Jean-Pierre Liégeois, 59–88. Hatfield, U.K.: University of Hertfordshire Press, 1999.

Islam, M. Rafiqul, and Jahid H. Bhuiyan. *An Introduction to International Refugee Law*. Leiden, Netherlands: Martinus Nijhoff Publishers, 2013.

Jacobsen, Katja L. "Experimentation in Humanitarian Locations: UNHCR and Biometric Registration of Afghan Refugees." *Security Dialogue* 46, no. 2 (2015): 144–64. https://www.jstor.org/stable/26292335.

Kagan, Michael. "Assessment of Refugee Status Determination Procedure at UNHCR's Cairo Office 2001–2002." *Scholarly Works* 643, January 2002. https://scholars.law.unlv.edu/facpub/643.

Katz, Irit. "'The Common Camp': Temporary Settlements as a Spatio-Political Instrument in Israel-Palestine." *Journal of Architecture* 22, no. 1 (January 2017): 54–103. https://doi.org/10.1080/13602365.2016.1276095.

Keeler, Sarah. "Peacebuilding: The Performance and Politics of Trauma in Northern Iraq." In *The Post-Conflict Environment: Investigation and Critique*, ed. Daniel B. Monk and Jacob Mundy, 68–102. Ann Arbor: University of Michigan Press, 2014. https://doi.org/10.2307/j.ctt22p7hj9.7.

Koestler, Arthur. *Scum of the Earth*. 1941; repr., London: Eland, 2006.

Lindqvist, Ursula. "The Cultural Archive of the IKEA Store." *Space and Culture* 12, no. 1 (February 2009): 43–62. https://doi.org/10.1177/1206331208325599.

Loescher, Gil, Alexander Betts, and James Milner, eds. *The United Nations High Commissioner for Refugees (UNHCR): The Politics and Practice of Refugee Protection into the Twenty-First Century*. London: Routledge, 2008.

Loescher, Gil, James Milner, Edward Newman, and Gary G. Troeller, eds. *Protracted Refugee Situations: Political, Human Rights, and Security Implications*. Tokyo: United Nations University Press, 2008.

MacGregor, Marion. "Design for Refugees: When Does a Shelter Become a Home?" *InfoMigrants*, July 3, 2019. https://www.infomigrants.net/en/post/17921/design-for-refugees-when-does-a-shelter-become-a-home.

Mattsson, Helena, and Sven-Olov Wallenstein, eds. *Swedish Modernism: Architecture, Consumption, and the Welfare State*. London: Black Dog Publishing, 2010.

Monk, Daniel B. "The Art of Castramentation." *Assemblage* 36 (August 1998): 64–83. https://doi.org/10.2307/3171365.

Monk, Daniel B, and Andrew Herscher. "The New Universalism: Refuges and Refugees between Global History and Voucher Humanitarianism." *Grey Room* 61 (Fall 2015): 70–80.

Muhle, Maria. "A Genealogy of Biopolitics: The Notion of Life in Canguilhem and Foucault." In *The Government of Life: Foucault,*

Biopolitics, and Neoliberalism, ed. Vanessa Lemm and Miguel Vatter, 77–97. New York: Fordham University Press, 2014. https://doi.org/10 .2307/j.ctt13x00mw.9.

Murphy, Keith M. *Swedish Design: An Ethnography.* Ithaca, N.Y.: Cornell University Press, 2015.

National Immigrant Justice Center. "A Legacy of Injustice: The US Criminalization of Immigration," July 2020. https://immigrantjustice .org/sites/default/files/uploaded-files/no-content-type/2020-07/NIJC -Legacy-of-Injustice-report_2020-07-22_FINAL.pdf.

Nemser, Daniel. *Infrastructures of Race: Concentration and Biopolitics in Colonial Mexico.* Austin: University of Texas Press, 2017.

Nichols, Austin L., and Jon K. Maner. "The Good-Subject Effect: Investigating Participant Demand Characteristics." *Journal of General Psychology* 135, no. 2 (April 2008): 151–66. https://doi.org/10.3200 /GENP.135.2.151-166.

Norberg-Schulz, Christian. *Existence, Space & Architecture.* New York: Praeger, 1971.

———. *Genius Loci: Towards a Phenomenology of Architecture.* New York: Rizzoli, 1980.

Oliver, Kelly. *Carceral Humanitarianism: Logics of Refugee Detention.* Minneapolis: University of Minnesota Press, 2017.

Owens, Patricia A. "Xenophilia, Gender, and Sentimental Humanitarianism." *Alternatives* 29, no. 3 (June 2004): 285–304. https://doi.org/10.1177/030437540402900303.

———. *Economy of Force: Counterinsurgency and the Historical Rise of the Social.* Cambridge: Cambridge University Press, 2015.

Pallasmaa, Juhani. *The Eyes of the Skin: Architecture and the Senses.* Chichester, U.K.: Wiley-Academy, 2005.

———. *The Thinking Hand: Existential and Embodied Wisdom in Architecture.* Chichester, U.K.: Wiley, 2009.

Pasquetti, Silvia, Noemi Casati, and Romola Sanyal. "Law and Refugee Crises." *Annual Review of Law and Social Science* 15 (October 2019): 289–310. https://doi.org/10.1146/annurev -lawsocsci-101518-042609.

Pernot, Mathieu. *Un camp pour les bohémiens: Mémoires du camp d'internement pour nomades de Saliers.* Arles, France: Actes Sud, 2001.

Pestre, Élise. "Instrumentalizing the Refugee's Body through Evidence." *Recherches en psychanalyse* 14, no. 2 (2012): 147–54. https://doi.org/10 .3917/rep.014.0147a.

Pitzer, Andrea. *One Long Night: A Global History of Concentration Camps.* New York: Little, Brown and Company, 2017.

Raath, Andries W., and Hennie A. Strydom. "The Hague Conventions and the Anglo-Boer War." *South African Yearbook of International Law* 24 (1999): 149–65.

Rajaram, Prem K. "Humanitarianism and Representations of the Refugee." *Journal of Refugee Studies* 15, no. 3 (September 2002): 247–64. https://doi.org/10.1093/jrs/15.3.247.

Sassen, Saskia. *Expulsions: Brutality and Complexity in the Global Economy*. Cambridge, Mass.: The Belknap Press of Harvard University Press, 2014.

Schmoll, Markus. "Das Flüchtlingslager in Gmünd: Transformation und Authentizität," *Österreichische Zeitschrift für Kunst und Denkmalpflege* 69, nos. 3–4 (2015): 293–302.

Schwarz, Mario. "Architekt Heymann, Ingenieur Gröger und das k. k. Flüchtlingslager Oberhollabrunn." *Steine Sprechen* 46, no. 2 (2006): 8–16.

Scott-Smith, Tom and Mark E. Breeze, ed. Structures of Protection? Rethinking Refugee Shelter. New York: Berghann, 2020.

Siddiqi, Anooradha I. "Architecture Culture, Humanitarian Expertise: From the Tropics to Shelter, 1953–93." *Journal of the Society of Architectural Historians* 76, no. 3 (2017): 367–84. https://doi.org/10.1525/jsah.2017.76.3.367.

Sphere Project. *Humanitarian Charter and Minimum Standards in Disaster Response*. Geneva, Switzerland: Sphere Project, 1998. https://www.refworld.org/pdfid/3d64ad7b1.pdf.

———. *Humanitarian Charter and Minimum Standards in Humanitarian Response,* 2011 edition. Rugby, U.K.: Sphere Project, 2011. https://www.unhcr.org/uk/50b491b09.pdf.

Stevens, Dallal E. "What Do We Mean by Protection?" *International Journal on Minority and Group Rights* 20, no. 1 (January 2013): 233–62.

Stone, Dan. *Concentration Camps: A Short History*. Oxford: Oxford University Press, 2017.

Taylor, Charles. *Modern Social Imaginaries*. Durham, N.C.: Duke University Press, 2004.

Terne, Märta. "BetterShelter.org Presentation of the Better Shelter Product." Presentation at the Meeting of Colgate Benton Scholars with BetterShelter.org, Stockholm, May 31, 2018.

Thomson, S. J. *The Transvaal Burgher Camps, South Africa*. London: H. Rees, 1904.

"UNHCR's RSD Policy: Quick Guide." *RSD Watch* (blog). March 8, 2010. https://rsdwatch.com/unhcrs-rsd-policy-a-guide/.

Welton-Mitchell, Courtney. "Medical Evidence in Refugee Status Determination Procedures." *Refugee Legal Aid Information for Lawyers Representing Refugees Globally: Rights in Exile Programme:* (blog), n.d. https://www.refugeelegalaidinformation.org/medical-evidence-refugee-status-determination-procedures.

Whitaker, Brian. "20 Killed as Egyptian Police Evict Sudanese Protesters." *Guardian*, December 31, 2005. https://www.theguardian.com/world/2005/dec/31/sudan.brianwhitaker.

Zetter, Roger. "Shelter Provision and Settlement Policies for Refugees." In
    Studies on Emergencies and Disaster Relief 2, 29–98. Uppsala, Sweden:
    Nordiska Afrikainstitutet, 1995.
Zumthor, Peter. *Thinking Architecture*. Baden, Switzerland: Lars Müller, 1998.

(Continued from page iii)

Forerunners: Ideas First

Daniel Bertrand Monk is professor of geography and Middle Eastern studies at Colgate University, where he holds the George R. and Myra T. Cooley Chair in Peace and Conflict Studies. His books include *An Aesthetic Occupation: The Immediacy of Architecture and the Palestine Conflict.*

Andrew Herscher is associate professor of architecture at the University of Michigan. His books include *Violence Taking Place: The Architecture of the Kosovo Conflict.*